THE REL[...] STAR

A BIOGRAPHY OF
MALCOLM VAUGHAN
BY
EDWARD THOMAS

DVa

© Edward Thomas 2009
The Reluctant Star

ISBN 978-0-9540816-1-4

Published by DVa
10 The Quadrant
Eastbourne
East Sussex
BN21 2JU
England

A CIP catalogue record of this book
can be obtained from the British Library.

Book designed by Michael Walsh at
THE BETTER BOOK COMPANY
and printed by
ASHFORD COLOUR PRESS
Unit 600 Fareham Reach
Fareham Road
Gosport
Hants PO13 0FW

ACKNOWLEDGMENTS

Extract from *The Noel Coward Diaries*, Copyright © 1982, edited by Graham Payn and Sheridan Morley, reproduced by permission of Orion Books Ltd.

Extract from *Mind's Eye* by Basil Dean, published by Hutchinson. Reprinted by permission of The Random House Group Ltd.

The author is grateful to the following for information, anecdotes and background advice: Freda Bolton, Kenneth Earle, Maureen Gladman, Rex Graham, Kevin Lewis, Frances Line OBE, Jan Lynton, Dick Ray, Michael Thornton, Damon Vaughan, Daryl Vaughan, Gaye Vaughan, Michael Wild and Arthur Wyman. Most of all he is indebted to the subject of this book, M J Thomas, aka Malcolm Vaughan, not only for his memories but for the substantial record-keeping of his career, which proved invaluable.

CONTENTS

1

THE FIRST RUNGS OF THE LADDER

A late Monday afternoon; November 1957. Eight singers were on the London Palladium stage going through their paces at the dress rehearsal for the Royal Command Variety Performance a few hours away. They were standing behind the upright piano at which Herschel Henlere was seated.

One of the eight singers was Malcolm Vaughan. He looked either side of him at the rest of the troop, all in white tie and tails. On his right were Dickie Valentine and Denis Lotis. Stretching to his left were Ronnie Hilton, Teddy Johnson, Frankie Vaughan and David Whitfield. They launched into their act: a rendition of 'Alexander's Ragtime Band'.

They got quickly through the song, stepped to the front to bow to the royal box, empty and ready for the Queen's arrival. Then they marched smartly off, leaving the way clear for Max Bygraves, Count Basie and his Orchestra, Judy Garland and Mario Lanza among a hundred others.

In the long waiting time ahead, Malcolm reflected on the journey taken from no more than thirteen years earlier as a boy actor, when he was still called by his real name, Malcolm Thomas. It was then wartime London and he found himself playing kid brother to Richard Burton and Stanley Baker. But an even longer journey had begun from the start of it all.

Malcolm was the son of William Haydn Thomas who had been born into a Welsh farming family in 1903 but who would be destined, initially, for the exhaustion of underground pit life. William Thomas married Nancy, born in 1911, daughter of James Daley who had brought his family from Ireland to settle in Wales. Upon marrying William, Nancy was disowned by her family as they were staunch Roman Catholics whereas William Thomas was a traditional Welsh Baptist.

Malcolm James Thomas was born on 22 March 1929 at Abercynon. He recalls the pit where his father worked as one of the biggest in the valley and, despite the harshness, all the families living there seemed secure for life. A daughter was born to the Thomases who died as a baby but another surviving son, Clive, was born five years after Malcolm. In a local radio interview in the 1970s, Malcolm recalled the early mining days.

'I used to take sandwiches in a miner's tin that had a handle. That was when Dad worked on the open levels. It was the first time I remember the smell of the pits and I didn't like it. My dad used to meet me to take the food from me. Sometimes he would take me into the pit some two or three hundred yards. It got blacker and blacker and the damp acrid smell was awful. It still stays with me. But I s'pose as a youngster then it was something exciting, but looking back now, it was a tough game.

'But it was a very pleasant life in many ways. I recall the summer charabanc rides to the coast. It was a thrill to get to the coast, to places like Porthcawl or Mumbles, with all the neighbours and families together.'

A major change occurred when William Thomas escaped mining life. Malcolm again takes up the story.

'My father and mother decided to move to Troedyhiw near Merthyr Tydfil where we had a house in Yew Street. It was very pleasant there. We had a large garden and the railway ran along the back of it. Father then managed to obtain a job at our little station in the booking office, plus waving the trains in and out. It was a good village to live in and there were mountains either side.'

Malcolm told his Radio Cleveland audience in 1971 that Troedyhiw is pronounced Troy-de-roo and means 'the little village at the foot of the stream'.

'My dad and I used to go up the mountain either side of Troedyhiw and pick blueberries for Mum to make delicious blueberry tart.'

Although difficulties continued on the part of the Daleys towards the Thomases arising from the differing religious denominations of the two families, animosity appears not to have extended towards the grandchildren. Malcolm recalls vividly James Daley, a military man who had been a bandsman in the armed services in Ireland.

'Grandfather Daley ran a little cobbler's shop in the front of his house in Merthyr. I remember the smells of the leather and the old shoe last. He had an old trombone hanging up on the wall. I used to watch fascinated the leather being cut and the nails knocked in. He could knock the tiniest nail bang in one go while the rest of the nails were in his mouth. For my benefit he would pull down the old trombone and have a blow on it.'

Perhaps it was from his grandfather that Malcolm's interest in music emanated. Whatever the case, while at school he joined Mount Zion Church and it was there that his talent for singing was discovered. At a church Sunday school anniversary he sang his first solo, 'A Child's Prayer', with its first line: 'Will there be any stars in my crown?'

He was taken in hand by William Long, a family neighbour and church organist who insisted that the boy practise his 'boring scales', for which his charge was to be eternally grateful. Mr Long steered Malcolm through further solos and accompanied him when he sang in several other places of worship. It was not a case of the boy being driven against his will for he developed a true love of singing, glad to be in the choir and taking part in summer festivals.

Others in the community took note of and keen interest in Malcolm's singing. They included Ben Davies, precentor of Deml Chapel, Abercabaid. When he first heard the boy, Davies offered what was to be a well-founded prediction.

'Malcolm, my boy, you are gifted with a beautiful voice and if you will take care of yourself, I venture to forecast a successful career for you.'

A turn of events occurred in 1943. The Second World War had been raging for four years. Malcolm was finishing his time at Pentrebach Technical School and his parents sent him to pay a visit to his father's sister and brother-in-law in Reading. When the time came to return to Wales, the fourteen year-old wanted to stay with Aunt Minnie and Uncle Morgan. Making use of skills acquired at the technical school, he got himself a job at a motor engineering works in Queens Road in the Berkshire town. The career forecast by Ben

Davies looked as though it would have to be placed on hold. In the event it turned out to be not for long.

'When I first went to Reading I realised I desperately wanted to work in a garage: the dungarees, the overalls and the spanners. When I got the job my sole purpose was to fill up the tyres with air. I was thrilled to death with this but was there for no more than two months.'

Minnie Davies ran what Malcolm describes as an enormous guest house in Sidmouth Street where he became used to staying up late watching with fascination as his aunt played cards with her boarders, remembered as 'mainly Irish guys who were all delightful and worked hard'.

Mr and Mrs Davies had two daughters, Marian and Roselyn. Malcolm wondered why no mention was ever made of the son he knew they also had. It was to be some time before he was told that Raymond Davies had gone down with H.M.S. Hood, sunk by the Bismarck, two years before Malcolm's arrival at the family home. In common with many such bereaved families at the time, the loss was never discussed.

Aunt Minnie spotted an advertisement in one of the popular newspapers of the day, *Reynolds News*, which was to set Malcolm on his show business path. Writing on behalf of Emlyn Williams, the journalist David Raymond made an appeal for a Welsh schoolboy, about fourteen years old and not over five feet in height. He was wanted for a new comedy written by Williams entitled *The Druid's Rest*. Without telling Malcolm, his aunt replied to the advertisement. Some weeks later they were both invited to meet Emlyn Williams at the Globe (now Gielgud) Theatre, Shaftesbury Avenue. The Globe housed the head office of H.M. Tennent Ltd, then the biggest production company in the West End. Malcolm felt a sense of trepidation as he and his aunt were taken up in the lift to the top floor, but once introduced to the famous Welsh writer and actor, all nervousness evaporated. Williams spoke in the soft lilting dialect of North Wales, which put the boy immediately at ease. Williams asked Malcolm to read a passage then chatted about travelling on tour and tested Malcolm's thoughts. The boy was eager to get on with all of it.

11 October 1943 was the date Malcolm Thomas was engaged for his first theatre job and today at his home in Eastbourne he still has the relevant letter of confirmation signed by Hugh (Binkie) Beaumont. Rehearsals began later the same month and *The Druid's Rest* opened at the Theatre Royal, Nottingham on 22 November. His salary was £7 a week for eight performances – a whopping amount for a fourteen year-old in wartime. Aunt Minnie was reassured by the General Manager of Tennents that Malcolm would be looked after. He and the other boy in the cast, Brynmor Thomas, would be attended to by a matron, Mrs Biddiscombe, wife of one of the members of staff and 'a very reliable person who will see to their accommodation, meals, and will naturally keep a proper account of the weekly living expenses of the boys and draw this from each boy each week'.

Further excitement was to follow even before the play reached the West End. Emlyn Williams arranged to take a company to play in Cairo for the Department of National Service Entertainment (ENSA). Malcolm's father in South Wales agreed that the boy could go with them, his mother having died prematurely during the UK tour. Another letter signed by Binkie Beaumont confirmed the arrangement 'whereby Malcolm Thomas will play in the season of plays at the Opera House, Cairo for a period of six weeks'. Four plays would be presented and specifically Malcolm would be playing Tommos in *The Druid's Rest* and understudy the part of Percy in Terence Rattigan's *Flare Path*.

By good fortune the pre-London tour took the play to the Empire Theatre, Swansea and the Prince of Wales Theatre, Cardiff consecutively over the Christmas and New Year period. Consequently Malcolm was able to return home for two weekends for his first meetings with his father and brother Clive since Nancy Thomas' death at the age of 32 in the November. They could not have been easy Christmas visits.

Two other members of the cast were also able to reunite with their Welsh roots. Richard Burton was making his professional debut, playing the part of Glan, in *The Druid's Rest* and saw his family at their home near Port Talbot.

Stanley Baker made a similar Christmas visit to his parental home where by a quirk of life's coincidences, a member of the current writer's own family was installed. An aunt, and her young son by a previous marriage, had been evacuated from east London and billeted in the home of Mrs Elizabeth Baker and her husband. In the post-war years of the late Forties, after the aunt had returned home to Stoke Newington, she and the author's uncle were able to return the favour of the occasional meal to Stanley Baker, then in lean years until he caught up with his friend Richard Burton in the stardom stakes.

Stanley Baker

photo taken by Malcolm Thomas on the roof of St Martin's Theatre, London 1943

Malcolm was learning fast about theatre life: both its heartaches and its requirements. Company Manager for Tennents, Frank Freeman, wrote a weekly letter to Mrs Davies at Reading giving an account of the money passed to Malcolm, the balance to come to his aunt. On 11 December 1943, from the play's venue for the week, the King's Theatre, Southsea, Freeman wrote: 'I have pleasure in forwarding the balance of Malcolm's salary; you will please note that he has had an extra 12/6 (63p) this week as he very rightly wanted to pay his Actors' Equity subscription; I trust you are in agreement?'

In January 1944 *The Druid's Rest* began its run at the St Martin's Theatre, London where Malcolm understudied until the departure for Egypt on 1 February. It was the middle of March before the company returned from Malcolm's first trip abroad.

As soon as it was clear that Malcolm was to stay at Reading and embark on a theatre career, Aunt Minnie had shown foresight in organising Malcolm with a local singing teacher following his return from the Middle East. Madame Des Agnes had been trained by Dame Nellie Melba and been a member of the Carl Rosa Opera Company. She taught Malcolm about breath control. Everything must start at the pit of the diaphragm. Malcolm learned that as a singer he must give his all and still have something in reserve at the end of the song. When the run of *The Druid's Rest* ended, Malcolm was well geared to auditioning for a big new musical soon to be opening in the West End. Added to which, another guiding force was exerting its influence.

One of the cast of the Emlyn Williams play was the eminent actor Michael Shepley. As the play approached its final week at the St Martin's Theatre, Shepley asked Malcolm: 'Now, young man, do you have an agent?'

When he said no, Shepley went on: 'We must get one and I will fix that for you.'

He took Malcolm to meet Gordon Harbord: 'a distinguished-looking Englishman with a handlebar moustache.' Harbord was already the agent for George Black. 'And that's how', reports Malcolm, 'I was called to the London Hippodrome, a stone's throw from Harbord's office in St Martin's Lane to sing for a man called Debroy Somers. So I went and sang "I'll Walk Beside You". That's how I landed the part of David in *Jenny Jones*.'

On 18 August 1944 Mrs Davies, on Malcolm's behalf, signed a contract with Beta Productions, based at Great Missenden, for him to play the part at the rate of £12 per week.

2

CHILD STAR

Jenny Jones, book by Ronald Gow, music by Harry Parr Davies, presented by George Black, opened in October 1944. Among the cast were Jimmy James, Pat Lancaster and Ronald Millar (forty years before the latter became Mrs Thatcher's speech writer and produced the phrase: 'The lady's not for turning').

Nearly six decades later Malcolm Vaughan vividly recalled the effect of the first night on him in conversation with John Hannam for Isle of Wight Radio.

'On opening night I sang the song "My Wish" leaning over the banister of a staircase with Ronald Millar playing the piano for me. I just sang it as we'd rehearsed and of course I'd never experienced anything like it in the whole of my young life. The place erupted and I had to sing it three times before they would let me go off, which was wonderful.'

The critics agreed. The usually acerbic James Agate reserved his praise for the lad from the Rhondda in his *Sunday Times* review.

> There was a nice little boy called Malcolm Thomas, who was allowed to talk too much and sing too little. His is the pure treble of the choir boy. Constructive as ever, 1 suggest that Mr Black should sacrifice several chunks of the plot, let down a velvet curtain and send on Master Thomas to discourse on 'Angels Ever Bright and Fair' and other cherubim and seraphim.

Playing the title role, the future Lady Delfont was livid. Her own notice from James Agate was somewhat in contrast.

> Some compensation was afforded by Miss Carole Lynn *(even misspelling her name from the correct Lynne)* whose singing appeared to know nothing between an ultimate pianissimo and a piercing shriek of which Euston had been jealous.

Malcolm received universal praise from all who wrote of *Jenny Jones*. Said A E Wilson in the London evening paper, *The Star*: 'The outstanding hit, in fact, is made by the boy actor, Malcolm Thomas, whose treble voice has great sweetness.' Indeed Wilson headlined his review with the words: BOY TRIUMPHS IN NEW PLAY.

The *News Chronicle* stated:

A small boy from Merthyr Tydfil, Malcolm Thomas, quite definitely knows how to act and has a haunting singing voice, which is not used to its full advantage.

The *Daily Herald* declared:

Biggest personal success was Malcolm Thomas, a sweetly-singing little boy.

None of it seemed to go to the boy's head, not even the accolade from the London *Evening Standard* on Saturday 7 October 1944 whose critic stated:

A small Welsh boy named Malcolm Thomas has such a hauntingly beautiful voice, with none of the ghostly hollow sound that characterises boy trebles, that he could have carried the show to success if the story had been written around him.

Not bad for a few first notices at the age of fifteen.

One audience member of the time, Arthur Wyman, continues more than sixty years later to enjoy a vivid memory of Malcolm's performance and in particular his rendition of the song, 'My Wish'. Mr Wyman's friend, the composer Michael Wild, creator of West End shows *Maggie* and *Little Lord Fauntleroy*, was also a pupil of Madame Des Agnes at the time and was destined to take over the part of David in the event of Malcolm's voice breaking. His voice did not break during the run of the show so Michael Wild never did get his chance.

LONDON HIPPODROME

GEORGE BLACK

PRESENTS

"Jenny Jones"

♦

PROGRAMME

LONDON HIPPODROME

Licensed by the Lord Chamberlain

Proprietors	MOSS EMPIRES LTD.
Chairman	R. H. GILLESPIE
Managing Director	GEORGE BLACK
Manager	KENNETH SKEET

NIGHTLY at 6.15
Matinees — WEDNES., THURS. and SATS. at 2.30

GEORGE BLACK
presents

"JENNY JONES"

A Musical Play by RONALD GOW

Adapted from Stories by RHYS DAVIES   Music by HARRY PARR DAVIES
Lyrics by HAROLD PURCELL   With WENDY TOYE DANCES
The Play directed by HUGH MILLER
Decor by GEORGE RAMON   Musical Adviser : DEBROY SOMERS

Characters in the order of their appearance :

David	MALCOLM THOMAS
Olwen	PEGGY PALMER
Richard	KEITH BECKETT
Blodwen	CLAUDIA HILL
Price Watt	BOBBY VERNON
A Miner	SYDNEY MONCKTON
Another Miner	PHILIP VENNER
Morgan Jones	SYDNEY BLAND
Jenny	MARY WATERMAN
Dilys	CAROLE LYNNE
Mrs. Watkin	NONA WYNNE
Aristotle Herbs	BALIOL HOLLOWAY
Hugh	ALAN DARLING
Gomer	CHARLES WHITELEY
Curigwen	DI BEALL
Shiela	SHIELA JORDAN
Elizabeth	PAT RAYE
Gwyneth	PAT LANCASTER
Bryn	FRANK GOODWIN
Mary	MARION PARNES
Myfanwy	JUNE HOWARD
Emryn	COLIN CLARKE
Megan	BERYL O'DELL
Penry	RONALD MILLAR
Mrs. Armstrong	BEATRICE BOARER
Ugolini	KURT WAGENER
Maria	WANDA FANE
Dai	DEERING WELLS
Jimmy Armstrong	JIMMY JAMES
Paul	ROBERT SYDNEY
St. Ceiriog	TOMMY LINDEN
A Film Writer	DIANA KING
The Bride	JEAN MAVIUS

VINCENT TILDSLEY'S MASTERSINGERS
Speciality by THE THREE WALLABIES

"Episode in Havannah" written by HAROLD PURCELL
Based upon an incident in "Royal William" by DORIS LESLIE

In spite of the excitement of the time, conversation with Malcolm today evinces memories not so much of the show as of conditions in getting to and from it. The war was at the stage when Adolph Hitler was sending across to Britain the devastating V1 rockets: the doodlebugs. Unmanned, they were notorious for heralding their arrival with a massive sound which the populace hoped would continue. The terror became immediate the moment the sound cut out. Then the rocket would fall and the bomb it was carrying would do its worst.

Malcolm's memory is of the daily train journeys between Reading and Paddington. Often the youngest passenger in the carriage, he, together with his fellow travellers, would keep their eyes skinned as they all peered out and up to see the devil machines coming through the skies. The most awesome experience was to behold a British Spitfire making its way to a V1 rocket and by some trick of miraculous manoeuvre, position itself under the device when it was over an open space and by tipping its wing nudge it as far out of harm's way as possible. As a boy Malcolm thought of it only as an excitement, straight out of 'Biggles' and other volumes of derring-do. When he talks of it today and reflects on the implications of the bravery of the pilots involved, he is inclined to become emotional.

Night time travel back to Reading took place largely in the pitch dark of the blackouts.

A further significant date occurred on 20 November 1944 when Malcolm officially signed his first contract with the agent Gordon Harbord, or rather his father did on his behalf, as the boy was well under 21. William Thomas was asked to sign a document that began:

> I desire you and hereby employ you to represent my son in this country and/or abroad as his Manager and personal Representative for a period of two years from the date hereof, but you have the right to extend this contract for a further three years after this period of two years if you so desire. I agree not to employ anyone else as aforesaid during the said period.

Malcolm now had the first Mr Ten Percent officially in his life. He had already had his first taste of radio when, earlier in the summer, he had appeared in a play entitled *Sunbeams in His Hat* on the Home Service. It was to be the first of two associations with the same producer: a leading poet of the day, Louis McNeice.

In the autumn *Jenny Jones* led to Malcolm Thomas' first two major broadcasts, both in quick succession. At 6.30 on the evening of Friday 24 November 1944 the BBC transmitted a long excerpt from the show in which Malcolm was appearing. Two nights later came *The Big Show*, a variety programme arranged by Vernon Harris and broadcast at 8.05 on the General Forces Programme. So prestigious was it that the programme boasted pride of place on the front cover of *Radio Times*. Malcolm found his photo there in company with those of Sid Field, Cicely Courtneidge, Arthur Askey, orchestra leader Van Phillips, and husband-and-wife team Eric Barker and Pearl Hackney. The compere was Jerry Desmonde and the show was broadcast from His Majesty's Theatre, Haymarket.

It is worth emphasising that this was 1940s wartime. Although a fledgling television service had opened in 1936, it was quickly shut down three years later at the start of hostilities. The wireless was to be the mainstay of home entertainment for many years. Nor was it the age of instant celebrity. Andy Warhol's observation that everybody would be famous for fifteen minutes was still decades away. Wannabes stayed wanting. No banal thicko airing his superficial platitudes would have been given voice, there being no equivalent of 'reality radio' to measure up to the puerile world of *Big Brother*. This very term would not venture on to the national scene for another five years, when George Orwell's disturbing novel *Nineteen Eighty-Four* was launched, in which Big Brother was a large menacing presence.

In 1944, therefore, an appearance on the wireless was something to be reckoned with. And it gave Malcolm Thomas his first national peak-time platform. Needless to say, his two radio appearances within almost as many days had no greater impact than on his home town, probably each inhabitant of which was glued to their respective wireless sets. That was certainly the case with Miss Edith Martin-Davies, Malcolm's one-time head teacher at Troedyrhiw Infants' School. On headed

'The Big Show'

Sunday, General Forces Programme at 8.5 p.m.
Wednesday, G.F.P. at 1.1 p.m. (recording)
Friday, Home Service at 9.30 p.m. (recording)

The photographs of some of the artists taking part are reproduced here : (left to right, top row) Sid Field, Cicely Courtneidge, and Arthur Askey; (bottom row) Van Phillips, who appears with his Concert Orchestra, Master Malcolm Thomas, and Eric Barker and Pearl Hackney. Also in the programme are Paula Green, the Stardusters directed by James Moody, and Jerry Desmonde as Master of Ceremonies. The show will be produced by Vernon Harris on the stage of His Majesty's Theatre, London, before an audience of Servicemen and Servicemen's wives.

8.5 ''THE BIG SHOW'
Arthur Askey, Cicely Courtneidge, Sid Field, Eric Barker and Pearl Hackney, Malcolm Thomas, Paula Green, the Stardusters, directed by James Moody, Van Phillips and his Concert Orchestra. Master of Ceremonies, Jerry Desmonde. Produced by Vernon Harris

front cover Radio Times

26 November 1944

notepaper of Merthyr Tydfil Education Committee, Miss Martin-Davies wrote to Malcolm on 29 November 1944.

Dear Malcolm,

I am writing on behalf of the teachers and children of the above school who have just heard your broadcast. We are all very proud of you and feel very grateful to the people who gave you this wonderful start.

I heard your broadcast in *Jenny Jones* on Friday evening and you were excellent. Many of the Troedyrhiw boys would like to change places with you and I hope you appreciate your good fortune. Mr Lumley *(headmaster of the upper school)* will write you later.

Some day we may have the chance to see *Jenny Jones* at the New Theatre, Cardiff. Congratulate your teacher on the quality of your singing – he has done a wonderful job. Next time you broadcast I should like to hear your old favourite, 'I'll Walk Beside You'.

Heartiest congratulations, Malcolm.

Edith Martin-Davies (Head Teacher)

Malcolm Thomas went into 1945, therefore, on the crest of the proverbial wave, yet in that, the final year of the Second World War, he began with a set-back. His radio appearances of two months earlier had made an impact and there was to be another to follow. Malcolm was booked for the first of a new series of shows entitled *Junk Junction*. The star of the show was the celebrated actor and comedian, Syd Walker.

Walker was born in Salford in 1886. After working as a clerk in a steamship company, he went on the stage, making his first appearance in 1905. Years of touring followed, throughout the First World War and beyond, until winning his first West End role: Guy Tabarie in *The Vagabond King* at the Gaiety Theatre in 1927. He starred in the musical *Love Laughs* at the London Hippodrome in 1935 and in the following year at the Theatre Royal, Drury Lane in *Rise And Shine* with Irene

Browne. Syd Walker became a fixture in the wartime radio comedy *Band Waggon* in which he played a dustman who, with government blessing, exhorted the nation to salvage all it could. (Conservation was a reality decades before the environmental lobby got hold of it.)

By the beginning of the new year, 1945, Syd Walker was an established star and was given his own radio series in which he would appear as a station-master. The scenario lent an irony of its own to Malcolm, given his father's own established position in the same job in Wales. *Radio Times* set the scene.

> After a journey up from Leamington Spa on a cold and frosty morning, standing all the way in the corridor, we can see a germ of common sense in the fantastic idea that is the basis of Syd Walker's new series of Wednesday programmes. Syd is coming back as a station-master of Junk Junction, where every week a train pulls into one of his platforms loaded with musicians and artists who tumble out and settle down in the waiting-room to entertain each other and listeners. Among the passengers for the first *soiree* will be Malcolm Thomas, the boy star of George Black's London Hippodrome show *Jenny Jones,* who will sing 'The Bells of Aberdovey'. You either like or don't like boy sopranos, but Malcolm's singing in the first of *The Big Shows* brought many appreciative letters from listeners. *Junk Junction* is on Wednesdays at 6.30pm on the Home Service, repeated the next day on the *G.F.P.*

Joining Malcolm in the first programme were to be Ernest Butcher, Miriam Ferros, Vera Lennox, Horace Percival and the Four Clubmen. Script would be by Loftus Wigram, music provided by 'a section of the Revue Orchestra', the show to be produced and directed by Ernest Longstaffe.

Malcolm Thomas was to experience his first disappointment in show business. In early January Syd Walker died suddenly at the age of 58 and the series was cancelled.

Malcolm continued in *Jenny Jones* until the show closed two weeks later at the London Hippodrome on Saturday 27 January after 153 performances. He was not out of work for long.

3

ON THE ROAD TO THE END OF THE WAR

February 1945. On Monday the 19th, and with a little under three months to go to VE Day, Malcolm Thomas began travelling in company with the comedian Hal Monty, a process that was to last for much of the year. Malcolm's first job away from the West End settled him in gently to the touring circuit, for the first date was at the Palace Theatre, Reading, a short distance from 3 Sidmouth Street, his home with Aunt Minnie and Uncle Morgan.

Variety Band Box played twice nightly at 5.50 and 7.50 with a Saturday matinee at 2.30. The customers were asked to 'Laugh and be happy with Hal Monty, the General Forces Favourite and Resident Comedian of the BBC Feature'. The name of the show was copied from the radio favourite of the time. Positioned first in the second line of the bill was 'The Sensational Boy Singer from *Jenny Jones* at the London Hippodrome, Malcolm Thomas'. The boy was to carry the epithet with him for a couple of years. In third position on the same second line billing was the statement: 'Tommy Trinder presents the Piano Prodigy Michael Austin'. About the same age as Malcolm, Michael was to become closely associated with him and in essence to become Malcolm's first professional partner. In large type at the foot of the bill was the announcement: 'Billy Reid and his Accordion Band with Dorothy Squires'.

Reid, a composer twelve years older than Squires, wrote a string of hits for her, beginning with 'Coming Home'. They lived together, as one paper expressed it, 'in tempestuous sin', until 1952 when the rockiest stage of their relationship coincided with her meeting Roger Moore. Another artist of the time, Freda Gardner, recalled the pair when, with her own husband, George Bolton, they toured together in the late 30s and early 40s. While Billy Reid and Dorothy Squires presented a facade of elegance to the rest of the world, Freda remembered the blazing rows between them. The language emanating

PALACE THEATRE
READING   TELEPHONE 3449   BOX OFFICE OPEN   10 to 8.30 p.m.

5.50   MONDAY, FEB. 19th   7.50
TWICE NIGHTLY
MATINEE ON SATURDAY at 2.30

LAUGH AND BE HAPPY WITH

HAL MONTY

THE GENERAL FORCES FAVOURITE   THE RESIDENT COMEDIAN OF **THE B.B.C. FEATURE**

VARIETY BAND BOX

The Sensational BOY SINGER from JENNY JONES at the LONDON HIPPODROME

MALCOLM THOMAS

TOPS IN TAPS AND TEMPO

EVE CLARE

TOMMY TRINDER presents THE FIANO PRODIGY

MICHAEL AUSTIN

MARIETTA DANCERS

CALIENTA and LOLITA
SIDEWALKS OF CUBA

| LAURIE ROSS | JACK Raw Laughter FINLAY | EVE LOVE |

MAYETTE
" MAID " FOR JUGGLING

BILLY REID AND HIS ACCORDIAN BAND WITH DOROTHY SQUIRES

TRIBE BROS., Ltd., London and St. Albans

February 1945

from behind the closed doors of their dressing room had the paint peeling off the walls – unusual, Freda observed, in the case of a female artist in those days.

The tour reached Nottingham on Monday 26 March 1945. The variable starting times for the twice-nightly performances during the last six weeks of the War provide a fascination of their own. From the 5.50 and 7.50 kick-offs at Reading, the Nottingham shows got going at 4.55 and 7.10. The lace-making fraternity clearly retired earlier to their beds.

Following the Nottingham week came a break of two weeks and Malcolm used the opportunity to make one of his increasingly rare visits back to Wales.

The tour continued but for a while metamorphosed into a more lavish show produced by Jack Hylton and brought to the Stoll Theatre, London. 'Monsewer' Eddie Gray was added to the star billing with Hal Monty. It opened on 29 April but Malcolm records that most of the critics were elsewhere. Starting the same night, at the London Hippodrome, was Ivor Novello's *Perchance to Dream*. Jack Hylton's show, entitled *Laugh Town Laugh,* nonetheless received the attentions of *The Stage* and *The Performer.* They gave it a mixed reception.

> A first class variety bill under the title of *Laugh Town Laugh* which Jack Hylton, its sponsor, calls 'a crazy medley of mirth', was produced at the Stoll on Saturday. It has Eddie Gray as prominent contributor, and he has plenty to do, with new material and gags, as well as his ever-popular juggling. Valerie Tandy could be given more to do. 'Winter Fantasy' is her most prominent musical number but she also scores in the sketch, 'Her Great Secret'. Hal Monty acts well in this too and is also seen in his two variety specialities. Syd and Max Harrison get plenty of fun out of their turn. In the 'Variety Bandbox' scena, there are Billy Reid and his band, with Dorothy Squires singing, Stephane Grappelli, the talented violinist, Michael Austin, a discovery of Tommy Trinder's – and a clever pianist – and the youthful singer from *Jenny Jones,* Malcolm Thomas.

That was *The Stage's* take on the matter. *The Performer* spoke thus:

When Eddie Gray has charge of the rather muddled proceedings in *Laugh Town Laugh,* it is good fun, but there are some dull moments in between. The show owes something – not much – to the old Palladium crazy entertainments, but the craziness lacks any sort of inspiration. Hal Monty wanders on and off the stage in a self-satisfied manner. Some of his lines, by the way, should be blue-pencilled. At the end Mr Monty introduces the 'Variety Bandbox' with Billy Reid's band, Malcolm Thomas, the boy singer, and other artists. To supplement the chorus there are the Four Pagolas, who add verve and rhythm to the spectacles.

No mention of Miss Squires or Monsieur Grappelli. You can't win them all.

Nine days after the opening came the day the nation and Europe had been waiting for. There would still be five months to go before the treatment meted out to allied forces by the Japanese in the Far East finished, but Tuesday 8 May was the day for the first of the year's celebrations to herald the end of the Second World War. The West End of London had plenty to offer towards the festivities. 16 year-old Malcolm Thomas and the rest of the cast were in an aptly named show for the sense of occasion. Surrounding their *Laugh Town Laugh* were, among many others, Tommy Trinder in *Happy And Glorious* at the Palladium, Vic Oliver in *The Night and The Music,* in preview stage at the Coliseum, Cyril Ritchard in *Gay Rosalinda* at the Palace, Hermione Baddeley in *Leslie Henson's Gaieties* at the Winter Garden and Sid Field in *Strike It Again* at the Prince of Wales.

Noel Coward captured the mood in his diary for that night.

I went along to the theatre *(the Duchess where* Blithe Spirit *was playing)* and had a drink with the company. We all had cold food and drinks at Winnie's *(Ashton)*: Joyce *(Carey)*, Lilian *(Braithwaite)*, Alfred and Lynn *(the Lunts)*, Dick *(Addinsell)* etc. We listened to the King's broadcast, then to Eisenhower, Monty and Alexander. Then I walked down the Mall and stood outside Buckingham Palace, which was floodlit. The crowd was stupendous. The King and Queen came out on the balcony, looking enchanting. We roared ourselves hoarse. After that I went to Chips Channon's 'open house' party which wasn't up to much. Walked home with Ivor *(Novello)*. I suppose this is the greatest day in our history.

4

ENTER THE OLIVIERS

The omens were not good as far as *Laugh Town Laugh* was concerned and the show ran for only a few weeks. Then it was back to the touring circuit and a reversion to the original *Variety Band Box* show. By Monday 16 July 1945 when the show opened at the Palace Theatre, Manchester, Billy Reid and Dorothy Squires had left the company. Their places were taken by Tommy Reilly and Frankie Still. Their billing matter included the words: 'After 5½ years as Prisoners of War we present …' *Variety Band Box* went on to a summer season at Morecambe.

Malcolm Thomas was about to experience the inevitable conversion of his voice. He would soon have to surrender 'the pure treble of the choirboy' observed by James Agate less than a year earlier. Malcolm recalls the moment when he became aware his voice was starting to break. It seems not to have occurred in the dramatic circumstances of such as David Hemmings who was singing the role of Miles in Benjamin Britten's *The Turn of the Screw* when his voice caved in and he was whisked away from the opera in mid-performance. Hemmings' loathing of his replacement was tempered only by the understudy's voice itself cracking after three weeks.

Malcolm Thomas' transition to his adult tenor voice trod a calmer path. He was on stage at the Empire, Glasgow singing 'Danny Boy' when the signs emerged. His training with Madame Des Agnes came in useful for he knew how to nurse his voice along. But he realised he could not continue for long in the transitional stage.

Malcolm explains: 'When my voice broke, my music teacher took me to a great throat surgeon, Dr Thurston in Harley Street. He advised that I do nothing for at least three or four weeks. He gave me medication and eventually, thank goodness, my voice came back.'

He was at an advantage in that he could return to the legitimate theatre, in which Emlyn Williams had given him the chance to begin nearly two years earlier.

Nevertheless, the pitfalls and disappointments of show business were already coming Malcolm's way, evinced in two letters of attempted encouragement from his agent Gordon Harbord. No longer in existence are the letters from Malcolm's father in the first case or from Aunt Minnie in the second that sparked the correspondence but the flavour of the replies is clear.

6 December 1945

Dear Mr Thomas,

Thanks for your letter. Actually the position about Malcolm at the moment is this. The Gordon Harker play has now been postponed until February and 'Treasure Island' unfortunately fell through because they are having Miss Jean Forbes Robertson to play the part because she once played Peter Pan, which we think is the most stupid piece of casting as Jim is a lively tom-boy for whom Malcolm was admirably suited.

Mr *(Harold)* Fielding was definitely interested in Malcolm for some concerts so I hope for news in that direction.

Tell Malcolm there is no need for him to worry about his future but there are always blank sort of patches when things don't come off.

4 February 1946

Dear Mrs Davies,

Thank you for your letter. I quite appreciate how worrying it is about Malcolm.

There is every possibility that we can get him the part of the boy when 'The Dancing Years' goes out again on tour in March.

Fielding is still interested in him but as you've no doubt seen by the papers, is busy with his law case and the fact that he's going to America to arrange with Frank Sinatra to come over here so that he's really not had time to think of Malcolm but promises to do so on his return.

I am afraid his accent lost him the job at Stratford which was most disappointing as otherwise they were very keen to have him. You'll appreciate how anxious I am to get him away from hearing Welsh and he's got a quick ear. I hope he'll get out of it as it was against him also with 'Treasure Island'. The Harker show is postponed but when that happens I think he's definitely all right for it but I don't expect this will be until April and I hope by that time he'll be on tour with 'The Dancing Years'.

I quite agree with you that it would be an awful tragedy for him to be wasted on doing a commercial job after such a good beginning but as you can point out to his father, lots of stars are out of work at the moment owing to the long runs of the present plays which prevent new productions. However, you can rest assured that I'll get him going as soon as possible.

The Gordon Harker show did not happen, nor the tour of *The Dancing Years.*

We should notice the reference to Malcolm's accent. Any similar suggestion today would incur the interest of the Human Rights Act.

Notwithstanding the somewhat gloomy prognosis, fortune was with him when cast in a series of plays that stretched over a period of eighteen months from the beginning of 1946. It began with a second wireless engagement produced by Louis McNeice who cast Malcolm in *The Dark Tower,* broadcast on the evening of 21 January on the BBC Home Service. Transmission time was 9.15 to 10.30pm and the three days of rehearsal were reflected in the fee outlined in Malcolm's BBC contract of 8 January.

Seven guineas (£7.35p) plus £1 subsistence allowance plus £1.2s.3d for 3 return fares Reading/London on 18th, 19th and 21st January.

For every repeat broadcast – described at the time as a 'mechanical reproduction' – Malcolm would receive £1.16s.9d. Such eventuality, therefore, would not cause his agent Gordon Harbord to get fat, his cut amounting to about 3s.8d. (*16p*).

Malcolm's first theatre play of the time was the contemporary favourite *Housemaster* by Ian Hay. It was presented by Arthur Lane Productions at the Grand Theatre and Opera House, Croydon on Monday 11 March 1946. It starred Joan White – who also produced – and Julian d'Albie. Way down the cast list was Betty Marsden as Rosemary Faringdon. Malcolm Thomas played the boy Travers.

In the vicissitudes of the theatre, Malcolm found himself at the top of the roller coaster again no more than a month later. Monday 22 April 1946 was the date that *Our Town* was seen for the first time in Britain, at the Royal Court Theatre, Liverpool. Malcolm Thomas was cast as Wally Webb in the movingly definitive picture of community life and death at the turn of the 20th century in the small town of Grover's Corners, New Hampshire.

Not everybody was captured by it at the start. A Liverpool newspaper reported:

> Thornton Wilder's play *Our Town* had its European premiere at the Royal Court Theatre, Liverpool last night. It is on its way to London and it was unfortunate that it lost much force because it was played to a holiday audience affected by apparently uncontrollable coughing.

Presented by Tennent Plays Ltd and Una Plays Ltd in association with the Arts Council of Great Britain and by arrangement with Howard Wyndham and Bronson Albery, *Our Town* opened at the New (now Noel Coward) Theatre, London on Tuesday 30 April 1946. The impression made in the capital was immediate. The *Daily Mail* critic wrote: 'In a startling last act Wilder gives two pictures of a funeral, at which are heard the thoughts of the dead and the words of the living.'

Elspeth Grant in the *Daily Sketch* said: 'This production by Jed Harris will affect you. It is a story of a little ordinary town which reflects life as it goes. Is there anyone who can say that they have felt every minute of the life they have lived, that they have savoured it as it should be savoured? Is there anyone who can dispute the peace and resignation of the dead? I do not know but Mr Wilder made me feel that we miss too much of life and fear too much of death.'

Malcolm Thomas had won himself into a highly prestigious project. Within months he was to move into a second from the pen of Thornton Wilder.

Meanwhile Malcolm was trying his hand at yet another branch of entertainment: the British film industry, then at its height. Audiences were booming, to the extent it has been estimated that in the immediate post-war period, one in five of the population made a visit to the cinema every week. Production in the studios was thriving and it was to one of these, Ealing, that Malcolm Thomas commuted daily for a few weeks in the late spring of 1946 while at night he appeared in *Our Town* in the West End.

Margaret Lockwood was one of the big screen's greatest British stars and another vehicle found for her was *Bedelia,* an adaptation of Vera Caspary's thriller. Hard on the heels of *The Wicked Lady,* Lockwood was cast to type, playing the Borgia role of a woman whose speciality was in murdering her husbands. Malcolm was cast as the Errand Boy who delivered a kitten to the Lockwood household. The kitten inadvertently took advantage of some poison and died. It was that part of the plot that led to Lockwood's exposure as the murderess. Malcolm found himself surrounded by cinema industry names of the time such as Anne Crawford, Ian Hunter, John Salew, Beatrice Varley and Barry K Barnes. The director was Lance Comfort. The film was released in Britain on 8 July 1946.

Margaret Lockwood appears to have been 'big' in America. The autumn of 1946 found *Bedelia* playing the Victoria Cinema in Times Square for several weeks with a blazing fifty-foot colour billboard spilling out on to Broadway.

It was not, however, the signalling start of a film career for Malcolm. He was to make only two more in subsequent years. But with other significant fish to fry that autumn, he was not too worried.

The Skin of Our Teeth had begun its British theatre life a year earlier and H M Tennent had decided to revive the Laurence Olivier production for the autumn of 1946. At the time the writer Henry Adler analysed Thornton Wilder's play by comparing it with *Our Town* which had created a marked impression on London audiences. Adler opined that whereas *Our Town* was the story of a family in the present

– that was if one could call the turn of the century 'the present' – *The Skin of Our Teeth* was the story of the human family at any time in history confronted by three main crises: the advent of the Ice Age, the corruption of prosperity, and the devastation of war.

Heady themes for Malcolm Thomas to get involved in and he was cast as Mammoth in the Ice Age scene. A decade later George Devine would form the English Stage Company; here he played the central role of Mr Antrobus. Malcolm has fond memories of Terry Morgan, only a few years older than himself and playing Henry. In later years Terence Morgan would become a leading figure on the silver screen. Someone who already was such a leading figure starred as Sabina in *The Skin of Our Teeth*. Only seven years earlier Vivien Leigh had won the much-coveted role of Scarlett O'Hara in the David O Selznick production, adapted from Margaret Mitchell's story of The Old South, *Gone With The Wind*. Miss Leigh was in her years at the top. Before too long she would be in Hollywood again, playing Blanche Dubois opposite Marlon Brando in *A Streetcar Named Desire*.

17 year-old Malcolm Thomas found himself in an exclusive band of people privy to the tensions between director and star.

'Olivier directed from the circle and used a microphone. Vivien would usually be a bit late, to say the least. She would come on with two cats. Olivier used to go spare at the sight of them. He would say: "Vivien, please do take the cats away. We want to rehearse." She would say: "But Larry, I do like to have them just for a little while." But he would say: "Vivien, please get the cats off the stage." Eventually she would stamp her feet and go off.'

The Skin of Our Teeth opened at the Piccadilly Theatre, London on Wednesday 11 September 1946 with a cast of twenty-seven covering a total of thirty-seven parts. It ran until Saturday 14 December. On the Wednesday of the final week a cast party was hosted by the Oliviers. One of Malcolm's treasured mementoes is a seven-by-five piece of blue Basildon Bond writing paper imprinted with the star's name and dated 3 December 1946. The message states: 'My dear Malcolm, Will you come to a party in the Stalls Bar on Wednesday 11th December?' Two simple signatures follow: Vivien, Larry.

PICCADILLY THEATRE

PICCADILLY CIRCUS, W.1 GERrard 4506-7

Licensed by the Lord Chamberlain to J. A. WEBB
Proprietors - - PICCADILLY THEATRE LTD.

TENNENT PLAYS LTD.

in association with

THE ARTS COUNCIL OF GREAT BRITAIN

By arrangement with

MICHAEL MYERBERG and LAURENCE OLIVIER PRODUCTIONS, LTD.

present

VIVIEN LEIGH

ESTHER SOMERS GEORGE DEVINE

and

ENA BURRILL

in

THE SKIN OF OUR TEETH

A History of Mankind in Comic Strip

by

THORNTON WILDER

Directed by LAURENCE OLIVIER

Decor by ROGER FURSE

Matinees : Wednesday and Saturday at 2.30

Evenings at 7 p.m.

TENNENT PLAYS LTD.

in association with

THE ARTS COUNCIL OF GREAT BRITAIN

By arrangement with

MICHAEL MYERBERG and LAURENCE OLIVIER PRODUCTIONS LTD.

present

The Skin Of Our Teeth

A History of Mankind in Comic Strip

By THORNTON WILDER

Characters in order of appearance :

Sabina	...	VIVIEN LEIGH
Mr. Fitzpatric		SIDNEY MONCKTON
Mrs. Antrobus	...	ESTHER SOMERS
Dinosaur		LEONARD MAGUIRE
Mammoth		MALCOLM THOMAS
Telegraph Boy ...	By arrangement with Marion Ross	... PETER THOMAS
Gladys	...	JANE WENHAM
Henry	...	TERRY MORGAN
Mr. Antrobus		GEORGE DEVINE
Doctor		ALAN SEDGWICK
Professor		JOHN MOLECEY
Judge		MAURICE BANNISTER
Homer	...	NORMAN WEBB
Miss E. Muse		ROSEMARY ROSS
Miss T. Muse		LUCILLE WALKER
Miss M. Muse		DAPHNE NEWTON
1st Usher		HATTAN DUPREZ
2nd Usher		PETER REYNOLDS
Theatre Commissionaire		MANVILLE TARRANT
Majorettes ... {		ROSEMARY ROSS
		GEORGINA JUMEL
		SYLVIA BROMLEY
Fortune Teller		ENA BURRILL
Chair Pushers {		MAURICE BANNISTER
		HATTAN DUPREZ
... By arrangement with Marion Ross		... PETER THOMAS

September 1946

5

FROM BOYHOOD TO SPUD BASHING

Two further theatre jobs remained for Malcolm Thomas before the call to another occupation that beset all able-bodied young men who reached the age of eighteen in the late 1940s: the call to 'get fell in'.

On Boxing Day 1946 Malcolm took up residence at the Winter Garden, Drury Lane (on the site of the present New London Theatre) for a production of *The Wizard of Oz*. It was produced by the legendary, and legendarily difficult, Basil Dean. According to Dean himself, he was at a crossroads in his career. The long years of running E.N.S.A. throughout the Second World War had come to an end. As he expressed it in his autobiography, *Mind's Eye,* 'the consequent removal of the heavy load of responsibility that I had been carrying for so long left me ill-prepared for the struggle to regain my rightful (*sic*) place in the theatre.' At short notice Dean found himself directing *The Wizard of Oz* which was presented by John McCormick who also designed the set and costumes. Among the cast were Raymond Lovell and, playing Wilma the Witch, Ellen Pollock.

Dean went on to explain in his book that when the production was announced, the rights had not been completely cleared with Metro-Goldwyn-Mayer, makers of the highly regarded film version released only seven years earlier. As a result he had difficulty in persuading the M.G.M. representative in London, Sam Eckman, that no harm would be done to their auspicious film property.

Basil Dean concluded on the result as follows.

Preparations were carried out at high speed and at the last possible moment. But all our last-minute effects came off, including the climax of the entertainment: the inflation of a large balloon, which rose some twenty feet into the air amid the excited cheers of the audiences of youngsters.

Walter Crisham, nimble-footed as ever, made a weirdly attractive Scarecrow, and Claude Hulbert as the cowardly Lion gave one of his typically shy, retiring performances that were always in contrast to the extrovert performances of brother Jack.

The familiar music was by Harold Arlen. John McCormick's wife Janet Green wrote the script, adapted from the musical play by Paul Tietjens. This is not without significance as her writing in years to come would follow an entirely different path. Janet Green became a thriller writer producing work of considerable impact on the British film industry, especially in her collaboration with the partnership of Michael Relph and Basil Dearden. They embarked on a number of films with social concerns which were scripted by Janet Green. Most notable were the Rank Organisation's *Sapphire* of 1959, dealing with a racial murder, and even more so *Victim* released in 1961, starring Dirk Bogarde and Sylvia Syms. Green's gift was in providing an entertaining script first. Any 'message' was subtle and placed second, unlike today's approach where the apparent need is to ram it down the collective throat. The message was therefore all the more effective. In the case of *Victim,* the vulnerability of homosexual men to blackmail was clearly drawn. It did not come out fighting for a change in the law but six years later 'acts between consenting adults' were decriminalised.

Janet Green's work also took her to Universal Studios, Hollywood, providing a taut script for Rex Harrison and Doris Day in *Midnight Lace,* itself adapted from her own stage play, *Matilda Shouted Fire.* It is not surprising that her script for *The Wizard of Oz* was regarded by Basil Dean as an effective adaptation of the screen version.

Malcolm Thomas played the Mayor of the Munchkins. It fell to him to sing 'The Lollipop Guild' and have the whole company join him. He recalls still the sheer enjoyment of the exercise.

The Wizard of Oz was staged during the cruellest winter the 20th century had known. Not only was the Arctic weather intense but coal was so scarce that the Minister of Power, Emmanuel Shinwell, had to inflict the harshest of fuel shortages on the nation. It was a wonder the theatre did any business at all. But Basil Dean's show lasted its course, ending on Saturday 22 March 1947, the day of Malcolm Thomas' eighteenth birthday.

One further stage job remained plus an unexpected brief film part that came Malcolm's way before the military took over his life.

Anyone familiar with Children's Hour on the BBC Home Service in the Forties and Fifties will recall The Toytown Adventures of Larry the Lamb, especially the 'baa-ing' of Derek McCulloch as Larry. McCulloch was better known as the nation's Uncle Mac throughout the Second World War. Addressing the youngsters evacuated all over the United Kingdom he would sign off with the comforting: 'Goodnight, children … everywhere.'

The stories by S G Hulme Beaman were so much a part of life at the time that impresario Archie A Shenburn decided to mount a stage version. He acquired the services of Hendrik Baker to write the script and to produce *The Cruise of the Toytown Belle*. The show came to fruition at the Granville Theatre, Walham Green on Monday 7 April 1947.

Malcolm Thomas played Dennis the Dachshund. Accompanying him, as Larry the Lamb, was Betty Blackler, then still only 17 years old. Like Malcolm she had won childhood acclaim with her first musical role, as Elizabeth in *Panama Hattie* starring Bebe Daniels at the Piccadilly Theatre in 1943.

Playing the Mayor of Toytown was the stately Raymond Rollett, a kindly giant of a man who would become a firm favourite of children's television programmes in the Fifties, eventually to end his life by his own hand in a London hotel.

There are no records to suggest that the play continued to other venues but it did capture the interest of BBC Television. Malcolm has little recollection of the event but a grainy photo exists showing him and Betty Blackler in costume on the set at Alexandra Palace studios on Sunday 11 May 1947. The show went out live from 4 to 5pm, the producer was Alex McCrindle and for the one performance only Malcolm received a hefty £21. In those still early days of the medium one channel only operated, for an hour in the afternoon and from 8.30 until ten o'clock in the evening – two and a half hours in total. It was a time when radio favourites were tried out on television

GRANVILLE THEATRE
WALHAM GREEN
On the Piccadilly Line
(Change Earl's Court)
14-96 buses pass Theatre

7 P.M. ONCE NIGHTLY 7 P.M.
MATINEES: THURS. & SAT. at 2-30 p.m.

FOR A SHORT SEASON—commencing MONDAY, APRIL 7th

A. A. SHENBURN PRESENTS THE FIRST STAGE VERSION OF THE FAMOUS B.B.C. STORIES THE

TOY TOWN ADVENTURES
OF
LARRY THE LAMB

By S. G. HULME BEAMAN.   Adapted by HENDRIK BAKER.

THE CRUISE OF THE TOY TOWN BELLE

LAWRENCE HANRAY   FRED ESSEX

RAYMOND ROLLETT

CLIFFORD BUCKTON   ANTHONY COPE

BETTY BLACKLER

MALCOLM THOMAS   VAN BOOLEN

JOHN DEVERELL

ROGER TRAFFORD   BLIGH CHESMOND   ALAN WELCH

PRODUCED BY HENDRIK BAKER

Box Office Fulham 3477   **Prices 7/6, 5/9, 3/6, 2/6, 1/6**

and on hearing of a stage version of Toytown, someone considered a transfer to the small screen might be an attractive proposition. The experiment seems not to have taken off.

There was just time to go from the small screen back to the large. During the run of *The Wizard of Oz* Malcolm received a letter from Film Rights Ltd, a motion picture agency advising him to attend for an interview at the Bushey Studios, Hertfordshire in the last week of March. In the depths of the 1947 winter he travelled from Reading to Paddington, then across London for another train to Watford followed by a bus to Bushey. With public transport in turmoil on account of the weather and fuel shortages, Malcolm was late for his appointment with a Mr Catling. However, he secured the part. It proved to be an unexpected bridge prior to and following his national service for the film was not released until after he was demobbed.

For indeed the time had come for Malcolm Thomas' longest work engagement thus far: two years in the army. Three months after his eighteenth birthday, as was the custom, he went off one Thursday morning – again the custom – to the delights of Catterick for six weeks of hard training as 21005584 Private Thomas M J. The world of show business would not see him back until the summer of 1949; that was always assuming it required his services again – not necessarily a guarantee when artists had to break off their careers for the sake of national service.

Raymond Rollett

photo taken by the author
outside BBC Lime Grove
Studios, March 1956

THE RELUCTANT STAR

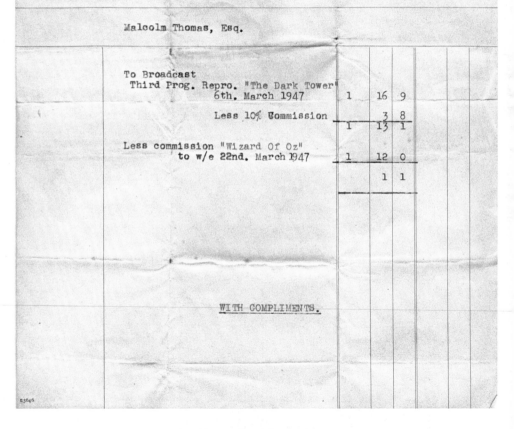

GORDON HARBORD

Theatrical Manager & Dramatic Agent

53 ST. MARTIN'S LANE,
LONDON, W.C.,2

18th. March 1947

Malcolm Thomas, Esq.

		£	s	d
To Broadcast Third Prog. Repro. "The Dark Tower" 6th. March 1947		1	16	9
Less 10% Commission			3	8
		1	13	1
Less commission "Wizard Of Oz" to w/e 22nd. March 1947		1	12	0
			1	1

WITH COMPLIMENTS.

Slim pickings for the artist

*Malcolm with
Brynmor Thomas
in*
The Druid's
Rest, *1943*

*Clive Thomas
— Malcolm's
brother.*

Fellow cast members,
Jenny Jones, *1944:*
(Clockwise, from top):
Jimmy James,
Sydney Monckton,
Carole Lynne.

*Malcolm on army leave,
Reading 1948 with his father,
William Haydn Thomas.*

*Malcolm, on right, with
Michael Austin and
another company member,
Morecambe, summer
1945.*

Malcolm with
Michael Austin,
1950

6

BACK TO CIVVY STREET

Malcolm Vaughan has little memory of his days in National Service. It was something to get through, as for any young man at the time. His six weeks' initial training was spent at Catterick Barracks, Yorkshire before he elected for the Royal Catering Corps. Following a year in England he sailed out to Athens in the summer of 1948 on the *Empress of Australia* and does recall vividly a bout of seasickness.

He was posted to Aliki, six miles from Athens. Between Greece and Egypt, the rest of his time passed peaceably enough.

June 1949 saw his return to Blighty and a new agent. The contract with Gordon Harbord had reached the end of its five years and Malcolm moved on to R G Blackie Ltd, a theatre agency in Shaftesbury Avenue in the heart of theatreland.

Before any theatre work came along, his second film was released. This was the film for which Malcolm had travelled to Bushey Studios in the hard winter of 1947 and which had apparently taken as long as his National Service to find a release date. Malcolm played Young Joe in A *Man's Affair,* which did not see the light of day until August 1949. Described in *Picturegoer* as a slight romantic comedy about a couple of young coalminers on holiday at Ramsgate, it represented a clear image of its period: a time when Kent still had coal mines and when people went to Ramsgate for their holidays. Indeed it was because they did that Malcolm was to enjoy a long summer season at the resort the following year. Among the cast of the film were Diana Decker, Wallas Eaton and Joan Dowling.

Malcolm managed a local Personal Appearance out of it. The manager of the Regal Cinema, Caversham wrote to say he would be showing the film on Thursday 3 November 1949 and invited Malcolm along as 'we have a nice stage here with a mike'. Irresistible. Malcolm was back in the public eye!

Immediately following the appearance on the cinema stage came one on television. The medium continued to be in its infancy and the producer Richard Afton was keen on presenting new talent. On the afternoon of Tuesday 22 November Malcolm appeared in a show called *New To You* which went out live from Alexandra Palace from 3.30 to 4 o'clock. He performed with his first professional partner.

It had been Gordon Harbord's intention to pair up Malcolm with a pianist and he had written to Malcolm as much as three years earlier to ask if Malcolm knew of 'a boy pianist' who would be interested in linking up in a double act. Indeed Malcolm did, for Michael Austin had worked in the same Hal Monty show and the revue spawned from that, *Laugh Town Laugh,* for Jack Hylton as the war had been coming to an end.

It was with Michael Austin that Malcolm appeared on television that November afternoon. They split the fee of sixteen guineas between them. The partnership was to last over to the following year's summer season. But before that, Malcolm Thomas developed another string to his bow: performing in an ice show, though without the rigours of having to balance on ice skates. His job was to provide voice-overs for the characters on the ice.

As Michael Thornton tells us in the journal of the British Music Hall Society, *Call Boy, Autumn 2005,* a considerable development in post-war show business was the sudden and massive popularity of revues, musicals and pantomimes presented on ice. The process had been helped pre-war by the success of the Hollywood films starring Sonja Henie, the Norwegian blonde who reigned as World Figure Skating Champion for ten consecutive years to 1936.

After the war ended, a boom in ice shows exploded in Britain with not only the two giant London arenas – Empire Pool, Wembley and Empress Hall, Earl's Court – packed to capacity, but also number one theatre dates throughout the country which surrendered to the swirl of skates.

Thus it was that Malcolm Thomas signed a contract in late November 1949 to appear in what was to be the first of several ice shows over two to three years. The presenter was Tom Arnold but it was with the Sports Stadium, Brighton that Malcolm signed up. In so doing, he was to reconnect with his past for it was Gerald Palmer who ran the complex and who devised and produced the show. Palmer was the husband of Madame Des Agnes, Malcolm's childhood singing teacher at Reading.

Malcolm opened in *Aladdin On Ice* on Boxing Day 1949 and the show ran until 21 January 1950.

A few days later he signed a contract to appear in the summer season show at the Granville Theatre, Ramsgate. The contract was for the pairing of Malcolm with Michael Austin at a rate of £40 per week for the two. It was a Tom Arnold show by arrangement with R G Blackie, scheduled to begin on 1 July. In the event the first night was Whit Saturday, 27 May. The management presents, declared the poster, *The Gay, New 1950 Edition of Summer Serenade*. It was devised and produced by Louis Barber. The season received national recognition when excerpts were included with other shows in Thanet and brought together in a programme entitled *Summer Showtime* which was broadcast from the Winter Gardens, Margate on the BBC Light Programme. The recording was transmitted on Friday 21 July 1950 for forty-five minutes from 8.45 in the evening. The show was produced by John Ellison, better known for his many years hosting *In Town Tonight*.

Because Malcolm Thomas and Michael Austin were a partnership for the purposes of the programme, the contract allowed for a fee of ten guineas to be shared between them.

BBC contracts were heavy-going in those days. They included the stark reminder: SONG PLUGGING IS BANNED AND WILL BE REGARDED AS A BREACH OF THE CONTRACT.

A note attached to the contract was even more forbidding.

Suspension from future broadcasting in BBC programmes, as well as the immediate 'fading out' of the remainder of your performance, will follow the interjection of any remarks, anecdotes or other material considered by the Corporation to be offensive, or any other unauthorised departure from the approved script, layout and running order of numbers.

In other ways evidence exists of the sense of decorum of the times. For example, a company called Ace Recorded Productions, run by

GRANVILLE THEATRE

Manager:
RUPERT J. COSTERTON, F.I.M.E.M.
EAST CLIFF, RAMSGATE
Telephone:
250

COMMENCING
WHIT SATURDAY, MAY 27th ✳ **NIGHTLY at 7.30**

R. G. BLACKIE by arrangement with TOM ARNOLD presents the

── GAY, NEW 1950 EDITION OF ──

SUMMER SERENADE

DEVISED & PRODUCED BY **LOUIS BARBER**

DANCES AND ENSEMBLES BY SHIRLEY COOK

AGNETTE & SILVIO
Famous Continental Dancers

SHEILA BENNETT
THE DELIGHTFUL SOPRANO

JACQUELINE DUNBAR
A NEW PERSONALITY

JACK
STANFORD
THE DANCING FOOL

3 IN HARMONY

EDWARD
ORLAND
WELCOME RETURN BY PUBLIC REQUEST

THE 6 STARLETS

MALCOLM THOMAS & MICHAEL AUSTIN
FAMOUS B.B.C. TELEVISION ARTISTES

JIMMIE LEE
Return of a Popular Comedian

MARION RIVERS
A GREAT FAVOURITE

ARTHUR
TAYLOR
FROM AUSTRALIA

J Lewis and P Bennett and based at 4 Denmark Street, London wrote to Malcolm on 14 July politely asking if the firm 'may have the pleasure of recording your broadcast in *Summer Showtime* on Friday 21 July?' Such letters are period pieces in these days of cassette tapes and mini-discs, not to say assumptions.

Another noticeable difference between then and now was the apparent profligacy of musicianship. The BBC radio contract contained the following observation.

> If you wish your act to be accompanied by the Corporation's orchestra you must provide the following band parts:
>
> Conductor (score or piano part); 3 violins; Viola; Cello (dbl guitar); Bass; Flute (dbl tenor sax, baritone sax & 4th clarinet); Oboe; 1st Clarinet (dbl 2nd alto sax & baritone sax); Bassoon (dbl tenor sax, baritone sax & 3rd clarinet); 2 Trumpets; Tenor Trombone; Piano; Drums. (17 parts in all.)

The summer season saw Malcolm through to the start of the autumn as was often the custom before the approach of the Christmas shows. It seems at that point that his association with Michael Austin came to a halt with the two going their separate ways. In years to come they would meet up again.

Meanwhile in late November Malcolm Thomas was signed up for his second ice show, to begin on Boxing Day 1950. Tom Arnold was presenting *Dick Whittington On Ice,* with Gerald Palmer again in charge at the Sports Stadium, Brighton. Toni Congdon was Alice, Valerie Moon was Dick Whittington and Evan King was Sarah the Cook. Playing Idle Jack was an American comedian making his debut in England, Johnny Melendez. For the second successive occasion the show took Malcolm into late January of the following year.

Which appears to have been a lean one. Malcolm Vaughan has retained all his contracts but there are no records of any work save one engagement between January and December 1951. Malcolm cannot remember the exact time but feels this could have been the period he became disillusioned and had a complete change of scene. With his background of a technical education and as a car mechanic, he somehow fetched up at Bristol and worked for an aircraft manufacturer. Romance came into his life acting as an incentive to stay in the west country. Not indefinitely, however. There is one recorded performance to suggest he was back in the metropolis by the autumn of 1951.

It was a Benefit in aid of the 'Lest We Forget' Association that took place at the Steadfast Sea Cadets Hall, Kingston-on-Thames on the afternoon of Wednesday 24 October. The programme consisted of 'Dinner *(sic)* at 1pm followed by Entertainment and Tea' and intended for 'Our War Disabled Ex-Service Guests'. The Second World War had been over for only six years. In the austere mood of the times, the menu told the gathering that Dinner would comprise 'Roast Meat, Potatoes various, and Greens'. How ominous that ingredient 'Greens' sounds now. The vision is conjured up of cabbage boiled almost to dish water. Raymond Postgate was only just beginning to make his mark at the time with the first of his 'The Good Food Guide'.

The show menu included Cecil Johnson – entertainer and compere, Victoria Cotton – entertainer at the piano, and Malcolm Thomas – Tenor.

The strange year ended with Malcolm's third successive ice show for Tom Arnold at Brighton taking him into a better hoped-for time. And indeed the situation did start looking up with the New Year, 1952. On 31 January another producing company came into Malcolm's life which would lead to a sea change in his career.

7

LIFE WITH OLD MOTHER RILEY

The production company with which Malcolm Thomas teamed up in January 1952 was run by the mild-mannered James Gaston and an extraordinary harridan of legendary fame, Rosemary Andree. Malcolm signed with them for a revue that would set out on the road on 17 March for an open-ended period.

Before that he was able to slot in an engagement of four weeks, for a late pantomime season – another on ice – beginning 4 February 1952. Although Malcolm cannot now recall the show details, there was a sudden temporary closing of the production almost as soon as it started. Two days after the opening, George VI died in his sleep at Sandringham and the new Queen was hurriedly returned from Kenya where she had been making a royal visit at the time of the King's death.

The management was Frederick A Gommer. At the top of the first page of the contract Malcolm wrote several years ago: 'Where I met for the first time Alan Weekes. Super guy; we worked together all the time on the ice show.'

And so to the Gaston & Andree tour. It opened on Monday 17 March at the Hippodrome, Ipswich. Entitled *Exotic Nights,* among the large cast were the double act, Eddie Davies and Max Lee, and Ellis Ashton.

In the show Malcolm Thomas found new partners. He teamed up with three other young men in the cast who became known as the Welsh Street Singers. Two of the other three were the brothers Bernard and Barry Johns, themselves a double act in the show.

The long arm of coincidence was to stretch far and wide. A full fifty-six years later, Malcolm's wife, Gaye, was frequenting a hairdresser's in Eastbourne. She was hearing about a man being cared for in a local nursing home. Only during the week of his death did it emerge that he was one of the brothers from way back, Barry Johns.

It transpired that Bernard had died two years earlier. Not having caught up with Barry in his lifetime, therefore, Gaye and Malcolm were able to attend his funeral and renew acquaintance with Barry Johns' first wife, Bambi. They also had the pleasure of meeting his widow, Maggie.

Back to 1952. Nomenclature seems to have played havoc in the Gaston & Andree world for by the time the show reached the Palace Theatre, Leicester on 19 May for a week, The Welsh Street Singers had been shortened to The Street Singers. Additionally, their bill matter declared them as 'Radio's Vocal Quintet' when there were no more than four of them. Furthermore, the show itself was given a change of name for the citizens of Leicester. It was now *Holidays with P(L)ay*. By the time the tour reached the Empire, Swansea on 30 June, the local paper described the vocal group as The Welsh Street Singers and as a quartet, while the billing still had them down as a quintet and the show had reverted to its first title, *Exotic Nights.*

Whatever the case, the four lads had not taken long to make their mark. The Swansea newspaper was in no doubt as to the leading performers of the show. Under the headline SUCCESS OF A QUARTET the reviewer wrote:

> Star attraction at the Empire Theatre this week in the revue 'Exotic Nights' is the quartet named the Welsh Street Singers. These young fellows can sing and may, in time, rival The Five Smith Brothers.
>
> Before March of this year they were individual singers in different shows. On joining 'Exotic Nights' they were formed into a quartet – with immediate success.
>
> Last night's performance was the first they had given in Wales and it seems they were a little afraid of the reception they would get. Whether they were born in Putney or Llanfairpwilgwyn, they need not have worried.

1952 was already proving to be more satisfying than the previous year. While the tour was in progress Malcolm Thomas signed two further contracts with Gaston & Andree within the space of nine days. The first was for the following Christmas season at the New Empire Theatre, Bristol. The second was for a revue to follow the

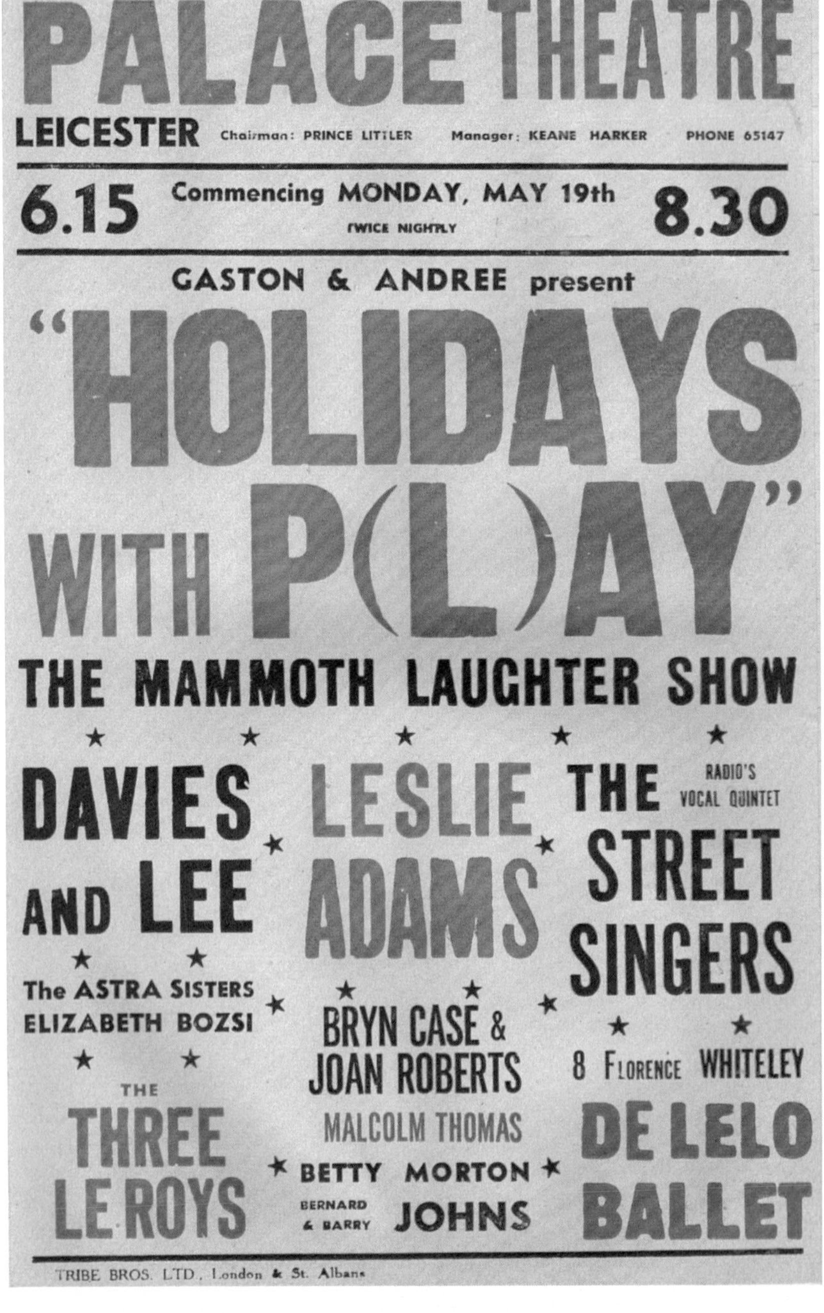
PALACE THEATRE
LEICESTER
Chairman: PRINCE LITTLER
Manager: KEANE HARKER
PHONE 65147
6.15
Commencing MONDAY, MAY 19th
TWICE NIGHTLY
8.30
GASTON & ANDREE present
"HOLIDAYS WITH P(L)AY"
THE MAMMOTH LAUGHTER SHOW
DAVIES AND LEE
LESLIE ADAMS
THE STREET SINGERS
RADIO'S VOCAL QUINTET
The ASTRA SISTERS
ELIZABETH BOZSI
BRYN CASE & JOAN ROBERTS
8 FLORENCE WHITELEY
THE THREE LE ROYS
MALCOLM THOMAS
BETTY MORTON
BERNARD & BARRY JOHNS
DE LELO BALLET
TRIBE BROS. LTD., London & St. Albans

May 1952

pantomime, starting in March 1953. Both shows would involve, as with the current one, solo billing as well as inclusion in The Street Singers (the 'Welsh' having been dropped, for the moment). Malcolm's rate of pay at the time was £15 per week. His agent, R G Blackie, wrote to him on 25 June 1952 as follows:

Dear Malcolm,

I don't know whether you want to accept the contract for the proposed engagement with Jimmy Gaston for revue to follow pantomime, but he is increasing your money by £2.10/-, and you might find it worthwhile to sign.

With the prospect of £17.10.0 a week, Malcolm signed. Meanwhile the present tour chugged on, to include venues such as the Empress, Brixton and the Palace, West Ham, with The Street Singers shown in ever bolder type on the posters.

Jack And the Beanstalk opened on Boxing Day 1952 at the New Empire Theatre, Bristol. The star of it was one Malcolm came to regard with affection: Arthur Lucan. It was the beginning of several productions the two shared. Malcolm became very fond of Arthur who adopted the nickname 'Chookey' for Malcolm. They would often have tea together and Arthur would give Malcolm valuable tips on comedy timing. In the dressing room Malcolm would watch in fascination as Arthur Lucan applied the face make-up for his character of Old Mother Riley.

Included in the bill was a double act, Macey and Mayne, whose presence would provide long-term implications for Malcolm's career, unforeseen for the moment. The quartet's billing continued to evidence its schizophrenic edge with some posters presenting the act as The Street Singers, others including the 'Welsh' tag.

With the panto season over, it was time to go on the road again. *Exotic Nights* and *Holidays with P(L)ay* were set aside and a new revue took its place. Given the only meaning attached to the adjective in 1953, the title *Going Gay* would have caused no particular comment, even with Old Mother Riley topping the bill. For so it was that Gaston & Andree continued to hire the great Arthur Lucan, accompanied by his partner, Roy Rolland. Macey and Mayne continued on the

NEW EMPIRE THEATRE · BRISTOL

Direction—F. J. Butterworth.
Phone. 209841

Res. Manager and Licensee—Kenneth J. Miles
Box Office Open Daily from 10 a.m. to 8 p.m.

TWICE DAILY AT 2-30 AND 7-0

Commencing Boxing Day, Dec. 26th for a Season

SENSATIONAL PANTOMIME ENGAGEMENT!

ARTHUR LUCAN

OLD MOTHER RILEY

IN

A Magnificent Spectacle of Laughter and Glamour

JACK AND THE BEANSTALK

PRESENTED BY GASTON & ANDREE
WITH AN ALL STAR CAST

SHEILA FRANCES   **SHIRLEY FYLES**
Principal Boy   Principal Girl

MACEY & MAYNE   3 DE LISLES   GALE DOUGLAS
Do-Little   Do-Less   Ivy Ginnochie
DOT & MAUREEN   MALCOLM THOMAS   BRYN CASE
BERNARD & BARRY JOHNS   NAN FRAZER   JOY DANCASTER

THE STREET SINGERS   THE PHANTOM GUARD
THE 10 FLORENCE WHITELEY GIRLS   PEGGY BARNES' LITTLE ALVETTES
Bristol's Own Tiny Tots

GRADE-ADA THE COW

| Box Seats: 6/-, 3/6 | Stalls: 6/-, 5/6, 4/6, 3/6, 2/6 | Circle: 6/-, 5/6 | BOOK EARLY |

SPECIAL CONCESSIONS FOR PARTIES

Christmas 1952

bill together with Malcolm Thomas and, in greater type still, The Street Singers.

Monday 1 June found the company playing the County Theatre, Haverford West and the next evening they did their bit to help the country celebrate the Coronation of Queen Elizabeth II, which had taken place in Westminster Abbey earlier in the day.

At the same time Malcolm came to know increasingly well one of the members making up the double act, Ken Macey and Billy Mayne. The real name of the first half of the comedy act was Charles Richards. He was from a show business tradition, his parents the jugglers, Percy Rich and Eva. Ken Macey and Malcolm Thomas eventually shared theatrical digs together and began talking of the possibility of teaming up in an act themselves. One suggestion was that comedy could be fused with Malcolm's singing. Ideas were bandied about as they consolidated their current work with Gaston & Andree.

A further contract for Malcolm was signed for the 1953/54 pantomime season even as *Going Gay* continued on the circuit, taking in the Opera House, Cheltenham in August and the Palace Theatre, Reading in September. It was during one of the 1953 weeks that Kenneth Earle – as Ken Macey became – remembers vividly a particular member of the audience.

Kitty McShane was the wife of Arthur Lucan. They had themselves been a double act with McShane acting the part of Old Mother Riley's daughter. Their relationship had always been one steeped in acrimony and even though they had officially parted, she continued to be Lucan's tormentor.

One day she caught up with the show and when Lucan was on stage, Kitty McShane stood up in the centre stalls to let forth a stream of invective against him. Gaston & Andree made it clear to all further theatre managers that the woman was never to be allowed in again. In the event Arthur Lucan was to have not long to live. A year later he was on stage at the Tivoli in his home town of Kingston-upon-Hull when he collapsed and died on 17 May 1954.

The Christmas pantomime of 1953 was therefore to be Lucan's last. *Old Mother Hubbard* opened on Christmas Eve at the Folkestone Pleasure Gardens along with Roy Rolland, Malcolm Thomas,

Macey and Mayne, Shirley Gordon, Cynthia Leslie and The Street Singers.

A summer week in 1953 proved significant: the settling of a name for the double act when it got going and a name of even longer-term significance for Malcolm Thomas. The tour of *Going Gay* reached the Royal Hippodrome Theatre, Eastbourne in the week beginning Monday 12 August.

The *Eastbourne Gazette* was especially taken with the quartet. 'The Street Singers' version of "Broken Hearted Clown" is a real winner', wrote the reviewer.

As was the established pattern by that stage, Kenneth Earle and Malcolm shared lodgings. By then increasingly serious about forming a double-act, they spent some time working out what to call themselves. While browsing around Eastbourne one day they spotted a sign over a shop. Some dispute exists as to whether it was a fishmonger's or a greengrocer's. What is not in question was the name over the shop: 'Vaughn' – without the second 'a'. They hit upon it at once. When the time came for them to get their act together, they would call themselves Earle and Vaughn. Their vision was one largely of a comedy twosome for nothing showed on the horizon that a major solo career awaited the new Malcolm Vaughn.

8

VAUGHN TO VAUGHAN

It wasn't easy. 'Earle and Vaughn' were established for officialdom purposes, including the tax man's, on 1 March 1954. The act was to last eighteen years, but for most of the first twelve months the story was one of hard slog around the music halls, which were themselves on a downward slope. That had started to be the position inland even if the scene around Britain's coast at the time was still thriving.

One example week that is recorded during Earle and Vaughn's first year was at the Palace Theatre, Halifax in February 1955. The description of the bill in the local newspaper typifies the style of variety fare that might seem to anyone under the age of forty to be out of the Ark. Included were the Two Jills, young dancers who in a double turn, said the reviewer, were 'attractively original'. The 'bumper programme' also included Marian Lane, 'who uses her fine voice to give realistic representations of well-known stars'. Winston Foxwell, the readers were told, was a novel juggler, 'and it is something of a surprise when he also becomes very entertaining as a ventriloquist'. There was the thrilling exhibition of 'absolute accuracy in shooting and knife throwing' by Cody who, with her partner Oran, displayed their varied skills in what they called 'Western Pastimes'. Lotus and Josie presented 'some tricky balancing while precariously perched on a swaying plank.'

Number two on the bill was Billie Anthony, a popular recording artist with Columbia Records, who had hits with 'This Ole House', 'Bell Bottom Blues' and 'Way Down Yonder in New Orleans'. Her inclusion on the bill reunited Malcolm with his first show business partner; by then pianist Michael Austin had become Billie Anthony's accompanist.

The star of the show 'just back from Australia' was singer and comedienne, Betty Driver, one of whose specialities towards the end of her act was to bring on her tiny white poodle, Mitsy. Miss Driver was to achieve even more national fame in later years by pulling pints nightly at the Rovers Return in *Coronation Street.*

Somewhere in the thick of this maelstrom was the embryonic act, Earle and Vaughn. The paper said the following about them.

Some modern fun makers combine action and dance, a little rough and tumble and song with their joking. These are the methods used by Earle and Vaughn with astonishing effect in their versatile double act.

Before the Big Time arrived, Malcolm was to characterise those first twelve months thus. 'We were just a double comedy act doing the rounds of the provincial music halls. We were doing all right but virtually staying as we were as far as advancement was concerned, when a certain week of variety came in for us. It was on that bill that the first of the breaks came along.'

The week in question was that beginning Monday 21 March 1955, the official first day of spring and one that turned the corner. Earle and Vaughn were appearing at the Chiswick Empire. Topping the bill was Alma Cogan. Also featured was the comedy disc jockey Jack Jackson who, Malcolm noted, had been 'a Santa Claus to many stars of the period'.

As part of the Earle and Vaughn double act, Malcolm performed an impression of the popular Italian singer, Mario Lanza. Jack Jackson liked it so much that he called Walter Ridley, the Artists and Recording manager at HMV and persuaded him to come and see the show.

Wally Ridley was also impressed, though not with the comedy act. Nor would he ever be won over by Earle & Vaughn. However, Vaughn on his own was a different matter. Malcolm had never sung in a recording studio but was about to do so; and for the first of many occasions.

Uncharacteristically though, Malcolm was physically sick with nerves on arrival at Abbey Road for his first recording. Nearly twenty-five years later Malcolm told Ian Charlton of Radio Cleveland about the experience on the programme *Dad's Music.*

'It was the first thing I ever did in a studio. I can almost feel it now and sense the thrill and excitement and the nerves and everything else. In those days you didn't record it in bits and pieces. There was a full thirty-piece orchestra. You would walk in and try to do it as well as you could and as quickly as you could, and as cheaply as you could. All done in two or three takes.'

Walter Ridley gave him the song 'Mama', intending it as a cover for David Whitfield's Decca version. Ridley arranged the B side, a song entitled 'Ev'ry Day of My Life'. The *New Musical Express* critic Geoffrey Everitt reviewed the record on 6 May 1955, confining his comments largely to 'Mama'. But it was the B side that took off and went into the charts where it stayed for sixteen weeks. The record also heralded one further and final change of name for the singer. On the record label, Malcolm's name was printed as 'Vaughan', with the inclusion of the second 'a'. Malcolm decided he had better keep it that way, thus his own style was set and the double act became Earle and Vaughan.

Suddenly Malcolm Vaughan was an overnight success, twelve years after entering the business. Patrick Doncaster writing in the *Daily Mirror* predicted a bright future.

> Once a week, sometimes more, I get breathless phone calls that go something like this: 'This boy's terrific! He's new, he's sensational! Another David Whitfield!' But these discoveries usually sound as much like David Whitfield as my Aunt Daisy. Until this week ... Along comes a boy with a big voice – Malcolm Vaughan.

Similar plaudits came from Scottish entertainer and broadcaster Rikki Fulton writing in the *Sunday Pictorial*:

> I've just been listening to the voice of Malcolm Vaughan. His strong clear tenor bends most pleasantly round 'Ev'ry Day of My Life', which has been given the usual immaculate backing we have come to expect from Frank Cordell. Malcolm is one half of a comedy act called Earle & Vaughan. If the comedy is as good as the singing, I for one will pop in when I see their name on the bill.

Their names were appearing on the bill with increasing frequency. Both artists were taken on by the Grade Organisation, specifically in the person of Denis Selinger, destined to become manager to Peter

Sellers and Michael Caine. Their comedy material was being provided by the up-and-coming writing partnership of Bob Monkhouse and Denis Goodwin. Malcolm's first record was swinging up the charts and at the same time the pair were on a summer circuit with Ken Morris and Joan Savage, Joan Hinde and, topping the bill, Ted Ray. In the week that 'Ev'ry Day of My Life' reached number 5 they were playing the Gaumont, Paignton and in the following week the Arcadia, Skegness. A month later found them at Eastbourne's Winter Garden, where the press were sticking to the first spelling of Malcolm's new name: 'Vaughn'.

It was not long before Malcolm was being asked now that he was on the road to a successful singing career, not whether but when he would be parting company with Kenneth Earle. He made his position clear as early as 1 July 1955 in the *New Musical Express*.

'My future is with the double act', he said. 'Both Ken and I believe in it. We're getting some good bookings. I'd be stupid if I broke up such a happy partnership.'

One of those bookings was their first television appearance together: *Variety Parade*, the peak-time Saturday night show on 25 June. Anyone who can still recall the variety programme will know that it was intended as a televisual version of music-hall: a succession of turns lasting a few minutes. There was no compere and as each act arrived, its name was announced in caption form at the foot of the screen.

Malcolm Vaughan was then firmly on HMV's books. Not all his records were hits but he was kept busy in the recording studios. By July his second disc was ready for release. 'I'd Never Forgive Myself' was coupled with 'The Last Rose Has Faded', orchestral accompaniments directed again by Frank Cordell. Then came 'More Than a Millionaire' coupled with 'Take Me Back Again'.

If 1954 had ended on a mediocre note, 1955's conclusion could not have provided a greater contrast. In December an edition of the national newspaper, the *Daily Herald*, summed up the dizzy show business story. It reported that when Earle & Vaughan had appeared at the Chiswick Empire at the beginning of the year, they were bottom of the bill. 'Last week,' said the *Herald*, 'they went back to the Chiswick Empire; to the top of the bill.'

The *Herald* recorded something else too. Malcolm's first record, 'Ev'ry Day of My Life' had by the end of the year sold 120,000 copies. His loyalty to his professional partner also became a matter of record.

> You know the comedy team of Earle and Vaughan. And you know (even better) the singer Malcolm Vaughan. It's the same Vaughan. And the point is, he feels he owes so much to his partner, Kenneth Earle, he is sharing his success with him fifty-fifty. Malcolm gets a penny a disc royalties and gives Kenneth a ha'penny.

Yet 1955 was not finished with Malcolm. It was the year his professional life turned around. It was the year his personal life did the same.

9

ROMANCE AND THE LONDON PALLADIUM

During one of the summer weeks of touring the country in 1955, Earle and Vaughan found themselves playing a week in Guernsey. In the course of the week, their manager, Denis Selinger, asked them to go with him across to Jersey to judge a beauty contest. They agreed and set off on the ferry to keep the appointment at Parkins Holiday Camp, later to be taken over by Pontins.

On a week's holiday at the camp were four teenage girls from south London. One of them had not wanted to go as she had been to the same venue for the two previous years and had planned to spread her wings. Her friends had managed to persuade her at the last minute to go back to Parkins a third time. The reluctant holiday-maker was further persuaded to enter the beauty contest and she paraded with the rest in bathing costumes. Earle and Vaughan and Denis Selinger elected her the winner. The girl's name was Gaye Hands. Kenneth Earle quickly renamed her Sad Feet, not without physical cause, aside from the play on words as Gaye recollects.

'I'd had an accident at the beginning of my holiday and my left foot was in plaster.'

Earle and Vaughan went back to Guernsey to complete their date in the show. Gaye Hands and her friends took up their workaday lives again at the end of their holiday.

One evening during the following autumn Gaye was at home in Tooting when the telephone rang. Her mother answered and called up the stairs: 'There's someone called Malcolm Vaughan for you.' Gaye said: 'Who?' Before the summer encounter she had never heard of the singer.

Malcolm was phoning from backstage at the Granada, Tooting where he and Kenneth Earle were appearing for the week in *The Billy Cotton Band Show*. Recollection returned to Gaye, and Malcolm asked her if she would meet him one evening after the show. She agreed.

To this day Gaye does not know how Malcolm managed to get hold of her telephone number. She takes up the ensuing story. 'We went by Tube up to Leicester Square and walked up to the Sabrina Coffee Bar. Over many a Cappuccino, which was just being introduced at the time, we talked and talked. Very late at night, after midnight, we caught the Tube back to Tooting, as you could in those days, and that was the start of it.'

The *Daily Mirror*, for whom Gaye coincidentally worked as a buyer, announced their engagement in the issue of 14 December 1955. Simultaneously the paper announced Kenneth Earle's engagement to dancer Barbara Willoughby.

No time for celebration presented itself, for immediately the pair had to leave their respective fiancees and rush north to Salford to begin rehearsals for their roles as the Chinese Policemen in *Aladdin* at the Windsor Theatre.

Malcolm plunged into the New Year with another release. The main song was 'With Your Love', backed up by 'Small Talk'. It was in the charts for three weeks but could not get above number 18. Made all too aware of the pitfalls of a pop career, Malcolm's determination to remain with his comedy partner was cemented. Their combined career was in top gear and both aspects of Malcolm's professional life were put to substantial advantage for two weeks in March 1956. It was to be his first engagement at the London Palladium.

As a contrast to the policy of introducing American stars at the world's leading entertainment venue, Val Parnell decided to bring together in one bill a host of home-grown artists for *The British Record Star Show*. The names, presented alphabetically on the poster, were Winifred Atwell, Kenny Baker, George and Bert Bernard (the only American act, standing in at a late stage for Jack Jackson), Petula Clark, Alma Cogan, The Stargazers, Malcolm Vaughan, David Whitfield and the compere. Tommy Trinder. Kenneth Earle was included for the comedy double act routine.

In order to gather such a force of talent for one show Val Parnell had to pay out £5,000 per week, and that did not include Mr Trinder's salary. Parnell gave himself another headache. As reported at the time the problem was: 'how to get a quart of stars into the pint pot of a

WINDSOR
THEATRE
SALFORD

FOR A SEASON COMMENCING 24th DECEMBER, 1955

JACK TAYLOR

presents

"ALADDIN"

Mortals :

ABANAZER	JON BODEN
WIDOW TWANKEY	DAVE MORRIS
ALADDIN	KATHRYN MOORE
THE CHINESE POLICEMEN	EARLE & VAUGHAN
WISHEE WASHEE	ANNE SMITH
EMPEROR OF CHINA	REX REED
GRAND VIZIER	REG RUSSELL
PRINCESS BALROUBADOUR	ALBERTA LAINE
CEDRIC	JOE GLADWIN

Immortals :

SLAVE OF THE RING	KARINA
SLAVE OF THE LAMP	RITA DELROY

Fairies, Butterflies, etc.

Specialities by

"SUSIE" :: REED & DELROY :: BALLADINIS

EARLE & VAUGHAN :: SLIM RHYDER

Christmas 1955

HERE'S THAT THRILLING VOICE AGAIN!

Photo : Derek Allen

MALCOLM VAUGHAN

WITH YOUR LOVE ★
SMALL TALK (from 'The Pajama Game')

POP130(78) 7M338(45)

10-inch Pop 78 r.p.m, 5/7d. inc. tax. 7-inch 45 r.p.m, 5/10d. inc. tax.

THE GRAMOPHONE COMPANY LTD.
RECORD DIVISION
8-11 GREAT CASTLE ST. LONDON, W.I

H1432/1155   Printed in Great Britain   K. & K.

January 1956

twice-nightly variety show – and do it without offending his record names'. David Whitfield clearly had ideas of his own on the subject when he expressed his candid feelings to a reporter.

'Look at me. I'm allowed just four songs and twelve minutes. Usually I do ten songs in half an hour.'

The unnamed reporter allegedly told Whitfield he was lucky and pointed out that some of the others had suffered more. For instance, the two youngsters, as he described Malcolm Vaughan and Kenneth Earle, got six minutes instead of their usual thirty-five. Petula Clark and Alma Cogan had diplomatically been given nine minutes each. Nor did it end with timings. Dressing room allocation proved even trickier. Who was to get the star room? Val Parnell solved it by having the plush number one dressing room partitioned into two. He installed Winifred Atwell in one half and Petula Clark in the other.

Beyond that, legend has it that Parnell was seen stomping the long Palladium corridors muttering repeatedly: 'Alphabetical order, alphabetical order.'

All the reviewers were preoccupied with the Britishness of the near entirety of the talent. Clifford Davis in the *Daily Mirror* enthused about the show, declaring David Whitfield, 'ex-£3 a week labourer', the hit of the show and he was glad that the cheers of the 'bobby-soxers' were aimed at Whitfield and not at visiting Americans 'as all too frequently in the past'. Davis went on:

> There was another good voice in Malcolm Vaughan who, with his partner, Kenneth Earle, threw in some amusing comedy spots.

Clifford Davis ended in some rapture that at last British variety had moved in to take over the world's top vaudeville theatre.

Cecil Wilson described the programme as Britain's answer to the American invasion of the London Palladium in a bill composed predominantly of 'home-grown gramophone favourites'. Writing in pre-politically correct days he described Miss Atwell as 'the coloured queen of boogie-woogie'. Emphasising her standing, he further spoke of her 'gleaming in a dress of gold, presumably to match her bank balance'.

In general the press was plunged into a belligerent show of defensiveness of British talent, as though breathing a sigh of relief that

March 1956

here was proof positive the Brits could hold their own as top-line entertainers. *The Performer* on 29 March 1956 summed up the mood.

Mr Parnell's great array of British topline recording stars began a two-week run at the Palladium to show that the cult of popular vocalism and instrumentalism is by no means an American monopoly and that home-grown vocal and instrumental talent, leavened by some fast-moving speciality acts, can evoke just as much enthusiasm as trans-Atlantic visitors.

Only John Balfour injected a note of caution. After likewise revering the Palladium's gradual reclamation from American artists by home-grown talent, he wrote: 'But it is sobering to consider that no fewer than seven top British acts must be assembled to fill the shrine'.

The engagement did wonders for Malcolm's solo career and for Earle & Vaughan. A talent scout from Germany was in the audience and wanted to snap the pair up. But he found himself able to book them for only the one week they had available for some time, fitting it around Central Television dates and a new variety tour scheduled soon to begin in Dudley.

Alma Cogan had a column in the *Sunday Mirror* which purported to feature her choices of latest discs. In the 15 April edition she greeted Malcolm's latest release as follows.

I like Malcolm's new HMV disc: 'I'll Be Near You'. It has simple, soothing, deep sincerity. Maybe that's because it's a wedding promise for Gaye. By the way, Gaye has a wedding promise for Malcolm too – no more beauty contests!

Miss Cogan raised the spectre yet again of the expected demise of Earle & Vaughan as a team. She reported that Malcolm had received tempting offers to appear exclusively as a solo act, but that he had refused to split from his partner. 'We're in this fifty-fifty and we stay that way' she quoted Malcolm as saying.

On Thursday 31 May the pair had a television date, in the prestigious *Startime* on ATV. A number of hectic tour dates continued but there was a special one looming a fortnight from the beginning of June.

10

BANNS

The minister at St Augustine's Church, Tooting was not easily won over. Malcolm Vaughan and Gaye Hands had gone to see him to book their wedding. 'We want it to take place on Sunday 17 June' was the request.

A Sunday? That is most unusual. Yes, but you see Malcolm works on Saturdays and it won't be possible that day. Well, I don't know. When was it you said? 17 June? I've got a number of christenings that day. The best I can do is to squeeze you in between two of them.

The vicar did not appreciate the implications. What transpired therefore proved to be something of a shock. He was not tuned in to the television news on the evening of Saturday 16 June. If he had been, he would have heard the announcement of the following day's nuptials and the service taking place at his church.

What he was aware of the next day was the huge crowd waiting outside. The town had turned out to spot the couple and the associated celebrities. Gaye and her father had difficulty in getting out of the car as the police held back the crowds. The vicar could not work it out. Inside the church the picture was the same: a packed house. If it had crossed his mind, he would have estimated the possible take in his collection plate when the time came for it to be passed round.

Malcolm's younger brother, Clive Thomas, was beside him as his Best Man. Present too was William Thomas, their father who by then had moved from South Wales to come and live with his younger son at Thornton Heath.

Wally Ridley from HMV was in the congregation to see his young protégé making his vows. So were various personalities of the day. Max Geldray from The Goon Show was in attendance along with Teddy Johnson – without his wife Pearl Carr who was doing some solo work. At the back of the church was Billie Anthony who Gaye still recalls being so emotional by the end of the service that when she and Malcolm proceeded out of the church, Gaye looked across to see Billie's mascara pouring down her face. Alongside her was her accompanist with whom Malcolm had first worked in the last year of the war eleven years earlier, and who had been his first working partner: Michael Austin, now restyled as Mike Baguley. Malcolm's current professional partner, Kenneth Earle was there along with singer Glen Mason and joint-head of the agency by then overseeing all Earle & Vaughan's work: Leslie Grade.

Streatham was a prestigious district at the time and could boast the Streatham Hill Theatre and the Locarno Ballroom. A third premier venue was the Stork Club, a leading cabaret night-spot, and it was to the Stork that the wedding party adjourned for the reception, leaving a still bemused vicar wondering why the occasion had evoked such enormous interest.

The local paper, the *Balham & Tooting Mercury,* did not share his doubts. In Monaco eight weeks earlier, the wedding had taken place between Prince Rainier and Grace Kelly. The *Mercury's* headline boasted:

'On Saturday Tooting had its own Royal Wedding'.

Following the reception a large group repaired to the home of Gaye's parents. At 8 o'clock in the evening the newlyweds made their way across to Liverpool Street Station. They took the train to Clacton, not for a honeymoon but so that Malcolm was *in situ* for the next week's engagement of Earle & Vaughan at the West Cliff Theatre. In fact there was no time for a honeymoon as work was keeping Malcolm at full stretch. The pair were in the middle of a long variety tour with Billie Anthony that would continue at the Hull Hippodrome and sundry other places.

For their first home base, Gaye and Malcolm found two rooms in a house at Victoria. Gaye still recalls the kitchen counter surface which lifted up to reveal the bath underneath.

The television dates became more fulsome. A prime-time Saturday night 9 o'clock spot of the time was *The Jimmy Wheeler Show.* On 7 July Earle & Vaughan shared the billing with fellow guest artists Thora Hird, Bryan Johnson, Marion Keene and the Fraser Hayes Four. Scripts were by Sid Colin and Talbot Rothwell (several years before

Sunday 17 June 1956

the latter started his *Carry On* days) and the orchestra was directed – as for any BBC variety show in those days – by Eric Robinson, brother of Stanford.

Further trips to Germany were fitted in to entertain at the British Forces camps. One of these took place in October 1956 and Gaye went along with her new husband. They stayed at the home in Cologne of Bill and Ruby Crozier. At the time Bill Crozier provided the German end of the highly popular Sunday lunch-time radio programme, *Two-Way Family Favourites*. Bill's co-host on the London link was Jean Metcalfe. Both Gaye and Malcolm found themselves the subjects of interviews with Bill Crozier on his own Forces radio programme.

Back home came more recording sessions at HMV. Gaye took on the habit of accompanying Malcolm to the recording studios at Abbey Road, St John's Wood and being mesmerised by the mass of glass partitions separating singer from the various sections of Frank Cordell's forty-strong orchestra. Press stories of the time that Malcolm could only perform love songs if Gaye was there so that he could look at her were, says Gaye now, just that: press stories.

In October, what would prove to be Malcolm Vaughan's most successful song to date was released. And everything was against it.

To begin with, recording artists had to rely mainly on radio for airings of their work. Television appearances there may have been, but song-plugging in the medium was frowned upon. If a record artist was booked for an appearance he was not expected to sing 'my latest recording'.

In any event, showcases specifically for young performers did not exist. *Top of the Pops* was not yet a twinkle in some television executive's eye. *Oh Boy* was not on the televisual scene, nor the Friday night *Ready, Steady, Go* – with its opening cry: 'The weekend starts here!' Much less available was the off-the-shelf technology of later years. The social mood also lent itself to certain restrictions. Coincidentally, one of these would be lifted within a few months.

In 1956 television went off the air between six and seven o'clock in the evening. According to the *Valentine Annual of 1959,* the newspapers called it the 'toddlers' truce hour'. The idea was that in that period the mothers of Britain could get their younger children to bed without the distraction of television.

In February 1957 came the revolution, in part. The cameras were allowed to open up at 6pm. Yet how would that new time slot be filled, in particular the Saturday evening hour?

At the BBC's Lime Grove Studios, Shepherd's Bush, a young man called Jack Good was taking a trainee producer's course. He had been to Oxford University, completed his National Service in the R.A.F., been a small part actor and social worker in London's East End.

He had also spent a precious shilling – precious because he was 'resting': the term used for out-of-work actors at the time – on seeing a film called *Rock Around the Clock* starring Bill Haley and the Comets. It was the first big rock 'n' roll movie, and it hit the screens of the world with a sensation then unheard of. It also hit young Jack Good with a thumping impact. Yet he was more impressed with what Bill Haley was doing to the largely teenage audience in the cinema.

'This is what the youngsters want; this is what we should be giving them on TV', he said aloud. He went back to Lime Grove and finished his course with one idea in mind: a teenage television show with plenty of rock, beat and excitement. He put the idea earnestly to the BBC top brass.

Uncharacteristically for the times they decided it might be something to fill the 6-7 hour on Saturday evenings and gave their consent. It happened that there was a young woman around with ideas similar to Jack Good's. Her name was Josephine Douglas, a Yorkshire girl who had been an actress but who was still best remembered as a panellist on the early Fifties television parlour game, *Find The Link* with Kenneth Horne, Carole Carr and Peter Noble. She too had taken a producer's course.

The BBC teamed up Jack Good and Jo Douglas. Between them they worked out a plan for a teenage programme and decided to call it *The Six-Five Special*.

It started slowly, not quite certain of itself. Then Jack and Jo invited the newest star of all on to the show: a thin, mop-haired, guitar-playing singer of rock numbers, Tommy Steele. The kids in the studio audience and millions of youngsters all over Britain yelled for more. Tommy Steele was invited back repeatedly to *The Six-Five Special*.

All that was in the future. In the middle of the 1950s only one television programme was dedicated to the latest recording work: Jack Payne's *Off The Record,* televised on alternate Monday nights. In an historical perspective the programme can now be seen as the first step taken to bring pop stars to the television screen.

The BBC's monopoly on viewing was stripped away in September 1955 with the introduction of ITV, when advertisements appeared for the first time. One of ITV's stars was Jack Jackson, the man responsible for Malcolm Vaughan's fame. He was given the late-night spot on Sundays and his programme became a must for the up-and-coming pop fans.

Consequently, at the time Malcolm set out, he was not able to do much backing up of his singing talent on the small screen. The appearances made in the medium were largely because of the other side of his professional life, his position as one half of Earle & Vaughan.

A booking to appear solo, therefore, on *Off The Record* on Monday 8 October 1956 was significant for Malcolm Vaughan, especially as he would have the opportunity to perform his latest release. It was called 'St Therese of the Roses'. But the appearance did not happen.

11

BANNED

Jack Payne had been a popular band leader in the 1930s and 40s. He was a forthright individual who pulled no punches in his responses to the new brand of pop singers. In his later television show, *Words And Music,* presented before an audience at the Television Theatre – now reverted to its original name, Shepherd's Bush Empire – he would lead the band and appear immaculate in white tie and tails. He readily applauded classical singers who appeared, but if he did not like a new pop singer, his hands would remain firmly at his sides.

According to Jack Payne's own account, Malcolm Vaughan requested of the producer of the television programme *Off The Record,* Bill Cotton Jnr, that he be allowed to sing his newest release. Jack Payne took up the story in his weekly record column.

> As many people already know, I don't like pseudo-religious songs and as this was a matter of principle, I expressed my concern.
>
> Bill and I asked Malcolm if he would sing the number on the other side of the record *(Love Me as Though There Were No Tomorrow),* but he declined. I think Malcolm and I understood each other's point of view.
>
> My attitude was supported officially a few days later when the BBC sound radio committee, which vets all popular songs, turned down 'St Therese of the Roses'.

And so the situation proved. The song was never heard on either BBC radio or television. Frank Patton, who published the song said: 'My complaint is that the sound radio people three years ago passed one which had much the same idea behind it. It was called "I'm Praying for St Christopher".'

Even Jack Payne admitted that at the same time as 'St Therese' was released, the BBC had passed Frankie Vaughan's record, 'Garden of Eden', which in Payne's view 'seems to deal with a matter less acceptable than that of "St Therese".'

When that point was put to a certain BBC executive, according to *Picturegoer* on 23 March 1957, the reply was: 'St Therese was a real person, but the story of the Garden of Eden is only a myth.'

The details were further elaborated the same month in *She Magazine*. The unnamed reporter had done some digging to find out who was responsible for banning 'St Therese' and discovered that it was a body entitled The Dance Music Policy Committee, which appeared to be centred in the Gramophone Department of the BBC under its director, Anna Instone. The reporter tracked down a spokesman, Douglas Lawrence, and tried to elicit more names but Lawrence resisted.

'It wouldn't be fair. It's a big responsibility to have to ban anything. In the case of "St Therese", I believe the decision was taken by Religious Broadcasting who thought it might offend a section of the public. Mostly, routine banning is concerned more with the introduction of trade names in American records.'

It had taken some time for even that elementary statement to be forthcoming. According to the *Daily Mirror* in the previous December, Frank Patton was still scratching his head. 'The BBC won't say why. There's no consistency'. Enlarging on his view Mr Patton said that he had played the record to his Catholic parish priest who had remarked: 'A wonderful song'.

The Catholic population of the Republic of Ireland thought the same apparently. Bert Newland of E.M.I. in Dublin told *Melody Maker:* 'We have sold over 7,000 copies, which is a record for a pop number in Ireland.'

On Sunday 4 November, Malcolm Vaughan was scheduled to appear on ITV's *Jack Jackson Show* with the Kaye Sisters 'and probably new rock 'n' roll artist Tommy Steele.' Malcolm had ITV's full permission to sing That Song on the programme. Then Radio Luxembourg hammered the disc for all it was worth. It seemed they had little choice. One of their DJs, Don Mason, reported that half the requests for his show for the months of November and December had been for the banned record. 'St Therese of the Roses' moved into the charts at number fourteen on 16 November 1956.

In a long article in the *New Musical Express* on Friday 14 December, Doug Geddes reported that with little opportunity to exploit the song, 'St Therese' had reached number 3 in the hit parade. The day before, the *Daily Mirror* reported that the song had by then sold nearly one third of a million copies. It was fast becoming a *cause celebre*. Malcolm had had no idea of the uproar that would ensue when he went into Abbey Road studios to record it. At the time it was just another job, and one that had not entirely captured his enthusiasm.

'I came down from Manchester to do the song. Ken and I were doing twice-nightly, so I had to make the journey to London and as I recall I was not feeling too good at the time.'

Today Malcolm continues to relish the fact that 'St Therese' was never overtaken in the charts by Elvis Presley's 'Hound Dog'.

Not that there was time to bathe in glory with so much work around. By coincidence part of it was to take Malcolm back to the scene of his greatest childhood glory.

Rising to the heights at the time was the comedian Dave King. He had his own show playing a season in the West End. Co-starring were Shani Wallis – the future Nancy in the film version of *Oliver* – and the ventriloquist Dennis Spicer, who would die tragically young in a road accident a few years later. Terry Scott also featured. During the run Dave King had to go into hospital suddenly for an operation. Benny Hill was hired as a hasty replacement but because of his own engagements Hill could not play the show for the whole period of Dave King's indisposition. The frantic producers called in Michael Bentine and also managed to nab Earle & Vaughan who themselves were within an ace of leaving for Bournemouth to fulfil their next pantomime engagement. They played for one week in *The Dave King Show* beginning Monday 10 December and Mr King returned the following week.

The producers were George and Alfred Black, sons of the George Black who had produced *Jenny Jones* twelve years earlier. They were thus able to bring back the child star of their father's show, the former

Malcolm Thomas, now one half of a top comedy act as well as having half a million record sales under his belt with his latest recording.

Malcolm experienced waves of nostalgia as he arrived to take part in *The Dave King Show* on the Monday in December 1956. The theatre in question was the London Hippodrome, scene of his war-time triumph as David in *Jenny Jones*.

Overleaf: The Dave King Show, *December 1956*

THE DAVE

OVERTURE   London Hippodrome Orchestra
under the direction of BOBBY HOWELL

" CLOWNS IN CLOVER "
(Music and Lyrics by Christopher Hodder-Williams)
(Décor and Costumes designed by Joan and David de Bethel)
Prologue   ..   ..   THE GEORGE MITCHELL SINGERS
The Clowns   ..   THE BALLERINAS and THE SHOWLADIES
PAUL WEBSTER   **PAT DAHL**
SHANI WALLIS

THE LOS GATOS TRIO   **TOPS IN ACROBATICS**

KENNETH EARLE & **MALCOLM VAUGHAN**
Radio & TV's Comedy and Vocal Team

" EASTERN MAGIC "   *(Music composed by Ronnie Hanmer)*
(a) The Kasbah   *(Designed by Alec Shanks)*
The Fire-eaters — **LES KAMERAS**
The Magician — **PAUL WEBSTER**
(b) The Magician's Dream   *(Designed by Erté)*

SHANI WALLIS   **"STRIKE UP THE BAND "**

TERRY SCOTT   **NEW STYLE FUNSTER**

" THE FOUNTAINS OF ROME "   *(Decor by Alec Shanks)*
(Costumes designed by Berkeley Sutcliffe)
Seeking Romance
WENDY BARKER   **HAZEL HEPWORTH**
and
JEANNETTE BISHOP
Goddess of the Fountain
LINDSEY ANDERSON
The Spirit of Romance — **PAUL WEBSTER**
—AND—
THE FOUNTAIN OF TREVI
Water effects by Jimmy Currie

INTERMISSION

ᴵ ᴺ ᴳ SHOW

"FASHION'S LATEST FOLLY"
(Music and Lyrics by Paddy Roberts)
(Costumes designed by Berkeley Sutcliffe)

La Mode .. .. PAT DAHL
Mannequins .. .. THE SHOWLADIES
Come Rain or Shine .. .. THE BALLERINAS

DENNIS SPICER with JAMES GREEN

TERRY SCOTT

HOWARD JONES and REGGIE ARNOLD

"ON WITH THE DANCE" *(Décor and Costumes designed by Erté)*

The Ballerinas   Pat Dahl
introducing
THE ANDREA DANCERS

MICHAEL BENTINE   THE ZANY COMEDIAN

"SYMPHONY IN PINK"
(Décor by Erté)
Costumes designed by Alec Shanks)
with
THE ENTIRE COMPANY

———

Dances and Ensembles by JOAN DAVIS
Orchestrations by RONNIE HANMER

Costumes executed by Alec Shanks Stage Costumes Ltd., Michel Mayfair and George
Black Ltd. Workrooms. Miss Shani Wallis's gowns in Scene 6 & 14 designed and made
by Sassoon Benjamin. Gentlemen's tailoring by Angel of Warwick Street and W. G.
Rossdale. Shoes by Anello and Davide. Wigs by Wig Creations. Sculptured headdresses by Hugh Skillen and Richard Dendy. Fluorescent headdresses by Frank
Winter. Scenery built by Brunskill & Loveday Ltd., painted by Alick Johnstone Ltd.
and Edward Delany. Metal scenery by J. Starkie Gardiner Ltd. Properties and masks
by Lovell and Drummond. Showladies' umbrellas by Kendall & Sons Ltd. Coloured
umbrellas by Grant Barnett & Co. Ltd. Nylon Stockings by Kayser.
Lighting equipment by The Strand Electric and Engineering Co. Ltd.

General Manager (for George Black Ltd.) .. .. HAROLD BOYES

Musical Director	For	.. ..	BOBBY HOWELL
Manager and Stage Manager	"THE	.. ..	EDWARD BEAUMONT
Assistant Stage Manager ..	DAVE KING	.. ..	COLIN WILLIAMS
Ballet Mistress	SHOW"	.. ..	SIDONIE DARRELL
Wardrobe Mistress	Company	.. ..	VERA OWEN

The British Record Star Show, *London Palladium, March, 1956
from left: The Stargazers, Winifred Atwell, Petula Clark, David Whitfield,
Alma Cogan, George and Bert Bernard, Malcolm Vaughan, Kenneth
Earle. Kneeling in front – Tommy Trinder.*

*Malcolm, Tommy Trinder, Kenneth Earle,
London Palladium, March, 1956.*

Tooting's 'royal wedding', Sunday 17 June 1956.

Fellow music hall performers: Wilson, Keppel and Betty.

Signing copies of 'St Therese of the Roses',
Beale's department store, Bournemouth,
January, 1957.

Opposite page:

Letter from Max Miller, 6 April 1957.

18, Charing Cross Road,
London. W.C.2.

April 6th 57.

Dear Malcolm,

As promised, - "The Tramp" Act.
Think my suggestion for opening is good, -
one in each corner, - paper over face -
cigarette coming through it, smoking.

Shall be at the 'Met' all next week, -
so if you are not working, perhaps you
will pop along one night, after Monday.

All the best,

In haste,

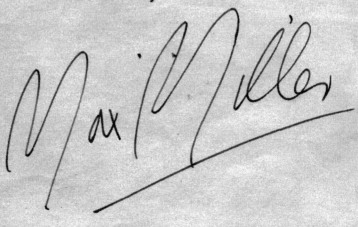

*Gaye and Malcolm
with Daryl,
October, 1957.*

*Publicity photo: Earle
& Vaughan.*

Front cover TV Mirror and Disc News, *1 June 1957.*

12

HALEY'S SUPPORTING COMETS

Malcolm Vaughan hit New Year 1957 running. Ensconced in pantomime at the New Royal Theatre, Bournemouth, with three performances a day on Saturdays, he and Kenneth Earle played the Broker's Men in *Cinderella*. Out of show hours there were personal appearances in department stores stacked with large piles of 'St Therese' copies to sign for fans, with the local press in attendance to record the event. One such record signing took place at Beale's, the big Bournemouth store of the time. The crowds flocked to catch a glimpse of this new heart-throb ballad singer.

Nor was it entirely possible throughout the run to stay in the south coast town to take the sea air for respite. Sunday 13 January demanded a trip to the capital to appear live on the nation's then favourite television show.

Sunday nights took on a routine in many homes of the time. It began at 7.30 with the matrimonial devices of Lucille Ball and Desi Arnaz in *I Love Lucy* and closed at 10 o'clock following a one-hour live play under the umbrella title *Armchair Theatre*. In the middle was another equally and very much live performance: Val Parnell's *Sunday Night at the London Palladium*. Because it was undertaken direct from the world's most famous theatre, it excited viewers who knew, every bit as much as those in the audience, that things could go wrong. It is testament to the expertise of all involved that anything rarely did. An appearance on the Palladium show, whether in the star spot or otherwise, would command an enormous audience. It is estimated that on one occasion in 1960 Max Bygraves drew in 20 million viewers. There were usually two or three acts before the first batch of advertisements. During the commercial break, the stage was set for 'Beat The Clock', in which people were brought up from the audience to compete in all sorts of physical and mental tests: getting half a dozen tennis balls into a bucket or rearranging the words of a well-known phrase or saying in twenty seconds. The winners, usually in pairs, would receive a prize. If time ran out, the compere would ask: 'Can you come back next week?' The curtains would close on the game show, the second lot of adverts would kick in and the crew would clear the stage ready for the last twelve minutes devoted to the top-of-the-bill spot. The late Jeremy Beadle once suggested that the television audience was more interested in 'Beat The Clock' than in the artistes appearing. Nonsense. Some of the finest performers were brought to mass British public attention for the first time through the Palladium show. In 1959 the then compere Bruce Forsyth asked the question: 'Can you come back next week?' of the current top-of-the-bill, Lena Horne. The audience went wild when she said yes.

Seasoned performers Earle & Vaughan took the date in their stride. Along with compere Tommy Trinder and 'Beat The Clock', they found themselves in company with Channing Pollock, Joan Heal and the cast of a popular London show then running, *Grab Me A Gondola*, and the star-topping Eartha Kitt, purring her way through 'An Old-fashioned Millionaire'.

By the start of the pantomime, Gaye and Malcolm Vaughan had moved up a notch in their domestic arrangements. They left their bath under the kitchen work surfaces in favour of a flat in Lingwell Road, Tooting, not far from Gaye's parental home. That too was to prove a temporary move. Bournemouth's sea air had performed its magic, for when they returned to London, Gaye was pregnant.

The pantomime at Bournemouth finished its season on Saturday 2 February. Yet again Earle & Vaughan scarcely had time to draw breath. The following Wednesday found them opening on a tour long-heralded and to be long-remembered for its significance as marking a seachange in entertainment.

Bill Haley and His Comets had been on the radar screen for a couple of years. They had first emerged in a song featured in the Hollywood film *Blackboard Jungle* starring Glenn Ford. The song was 'Rock Around the Clock'. Haley's reputation mounted in the United States until he made the film that took the title of his first success. It was the film which as already stated had so impressed the young television producer Jack Good. Reports reached Britain of riots

THE RELUCTANT STAR

erupting at Bill Haley's concerts, and cinema seats being ripped up at movie showings by out-of-hand teenagers. Hits had been made of 'Razzle, Dazzle', 'Shake, Rattle and Roll', 'Rip It Up', 'Rockin' Through The Rye', 'Don't Knock The Rock' and 'See You Later, Alligator'. The youngsters knew all the words. A fever pitch built up when it became known Bill Haley would be coming to do a tour of the United Kingdom. The equivalent of what came to be labelled Beatlemania a few years later descended on Britain in February 1957 when the liner *Queen Elizabeth* bringing Bill Haley and his Comets docked at Southampton. Sea voyages then still provided the more frequent form of travel from New York. Pandemonium broke out and the tabloids recorded every part of the arrival, including stepping on to the boat train and off again at Waterloo. It almost bore comparison with Chaplin's return from America in the early 1920s.

Following a couple of acts, Kenneth Earle and Malcolm Vaughan were to close the first half. The tour was to last several weeks and it began on Wednesday 6 February 1957 at the Dominion Cinema, Tottenham Court Road.

Uproar was the order inside and outside the theatre. The main support act benefited from what was happening. Reporter Mike Butcher wrote:

> The atmosphere was supercharged before Bill and the boys had even set foot onstage at the Dominion – so much so that we can sincerely compliment Vic Lewis and his Orchestra, Kenneth Earle and his comedy partner, HMV recording star Malcolm Vaughan, on their warm reception during the first half.

To this day Malcolm remembers the start of the second half: what he describes as the supersonic V-R-O-O-O-M-M-M heralding the arrival of the main event. 'The whole place erupted,' recalls Malcolm. 'It was the same every night of the tour.'

Patrick Doncaster detailed the scene for his *Daily Mirror* readers.

> The joint jumped! The floor vibrated. Bill Haley really rocked the place when he began his British tour at the Dominion,

Tottenham Court Road, London. Three thousand people clapped their hands and stamped their feet to the insistent beat of Rock 'n' Roll King Haley and his dynamic Comets. They sang with Bill. They roared: 'Go, man, go!' in rock idiom. They almost exploded.

For an hour beforehand we had the Vic Lewis Band, rockin', playing ballads; Desmond Lane, rockin' merrily on a tin whistle; the comedy-singing team of Earle and Vaughan. These two sang jazzy numbers, and Malcolm Vaughan gave us his semi-religious record hit, 'St Therese of the Roses'.

After reviewing the performance of the star and his group, Doncaster reported on the end of the show. He painted a picture of how things were in 1957 and, inadvertently, how they were to change.

The final curtain came down. The chant went up of 'We want Bill.' It died away as a recording of the National Anthem was played (*sic*). The audience trooped home. But not straight home. More than 1000 of them hurried to the stage door hoping to get a glimpse of King Rock.

In 2001 Malcolm recalled for John Hannam on Isle of Wight Radio that all the musicians on the Bill Haley tour were gleaned from top orchestras and big bands. He remembered the drummer, Ralph, who would be the first in the theatre wherever they were playing the tour and start practising as soon as he could.

'You'd hear him drumming away like crazy. Then he would throw his drumsticks down proclaiming: "Dammit. Why can't I play *good* music?".'

BILL HALEY And His COMETS
Decca Recording Artists

13

ROSES ALL THE WAY

Success bred success and it was reported that Earle and Vaughan's following was increased considerably by their participation in the Bill Haley tour. Hard on its heels came further variety dates at Finsbury Park and Nottingham.

All the while, Wally Ridley at HMV was not letting the grass grow under Malcolm's solo singing feet. In early March the successor to 'St Therese' was released. Because of his growing popularity, the new record was given the full publicity treatment including praise from a quarter that might seem incongruous today.

By 1957 Richard Attenborough was already widely known. He was a jobbing film star, whose name had appeared above the title ever since his portrayal of the sinister and sadistic Pinkie Brown in the adaptation of Graham Greene's *Brighton Rock* in the late Forties. With that exception, his deeper character studies still lay ahead of him; even more so his rise as a producer and director. The knighthood and installation as a peer of the Realm were decades distant. Though he had largely given up the theatre by then, Attenborough was equally well-known as a presenter of television programmes on history and music. Radio too continued to play a big part in his work. The host of the Monday night programme *Home At Eight,* which featured Hermione Gingold every week, he was also the presenter of *Your Hundred Best Tunes* long before Alan Keith came on the scene. Dickie Attenborough wrote a regular record column and he devoted one of them as follows, giving it the heading: MALCOLM IS A MODEL TO THEM ALL.

> When a young would-be player came to Tallulah Bankhead for advice, Tallulah let fall these acid drops of wisdom: 'If you really want to help the theatre, don't be an actress, darling. Be an audience'. Choosing my advice less destructively, my advice to any aspiring singers would be: don't try to copy the current American amateurs but listen to our own Malcolm

Vaughan. This 28 year-old hit parader has fourteen hard years in show business behind him. Throughout his professional career he has had only one thing to rely on: his talent. He has moulded himself on nobody but has been content to remain Malcolm Vaughan. He has toured the country in variety, doing a polished double act with his likeable partner Kenneth Earle. He has played in straight theatre, in panto and in ice shows. He has never been 'discovered' as such but he has blazed his own trail. He relies on his vocal chords, not an echo chamber, and his pure, expressive voice can fill a theatre without the aid of a mike. His recording company should cherish him.

This week I received his latest disc. One side has what I sincerely hope will be a prophetic title: 'The World Is Mine'. The reverse side completes the picture for the title is 'Now'. In both cases he has the able support of Frank Cordell and his Orchestra. The disc deserves to have an immediate and long-lasting success.

In fact 'The World Is Mine' did not set the music world alight and achieved no higher than a placing at 26 in the charts. Malcolm was unperturbed, his experience of the roller coaster style of show business life continuing to stand him in good stead. In any case another creditable success from the production studio at St John's Wood was around the corner.

'Chapel of the Roses' was released in May 1957. It was given a strong though honest boost by Keith Fordyce in the *New Musical Express*. Fordyce recognised the similarity in style and title to 'St Therese' but considered it no bad thing.

All I can say is that this cake tastes even better than the first one. If Malcolm doesn't prove to have another big winner with his latest, I shall consider it impossible to judge the taste of the unpredictable buying public – in other words, you! The religious flavour has soaked right through to the B side, 'Guardian Angel'. For my money this is by far the better title, an attractive lilting melody, and words that are in less questionable taste than 'Chapel'.

★ **HARRY BELAFONTE**
Mama Looka Boo Boo   POP339 (78 & 45)

★ **ALMA COGAN**
Chantez, Chantez   POP336 (78 & 45)

★ **RONNIE HILTON**
Around the World   POP338 (78 & 45)

★ **DON LANG** *and his 'Frantic Five'*
Rock-a-Billy   POP335 (78 & 45)

★ **SID PHILLIPS** *and his Band*
Everybody loves Pierre   POP341 (78 & 45)

★ **MALCOLM VAUGHAN**
Chapel of the Roses   POP325 (78 & 45)

"HIS MASTER'S VOICE"

for the TOPS in POPS

May 1957

Still, it looks like roses, roses all the way for Malcolm. Personally, I dislike religious lyrics in pop songs, and don't be kidded that these records are made for sentimental reasons. However, in fairness, I must add that some of these songs are put over in good taste, some in bad. Malcolm Vaughan's interpretations come into the 'good' category.

'Chapel of the Roses' reached up to number 13 in the hit parade.

There was one more visit to the HMV studios in 1957, in order to record 'Oh, My Papa', a vocal cover version of the massive instrumental hit by Eddie Calvert. It seemed though that the customers preferred the trumpet to the voice in that instance. Coupled with 'What is My Destiny', the record did not make it to the charts.

Not that Malcolm had time to worry. More television came his way in the form of another *Jack Jackson Show* on ATV. The company he kept on the evening of Sunday 7 April in the studio at Foley Street off Oxford Circus were Ronnie Hilton, Lorrae Desmond, Malcolm Mitchell, Glen Mason – one of the wedding guests the previous June – together with Joan Savage and Paddie O'Neil. Malcolm's diary records that he was paid £30 for the appearance.

The BBC was surprisingly a little more generous a month later when Malcolm received £32.10.0 (*£32.50p*) for an appearance that pleased him greatly. He had wanted desperately to appear on *The Six-Five Special,* and on Saturday 18 May he was given his chance.

The Six-Five Special had grown in popularity in only a few months, largely, it was thought in some circles, because of the regular appearances of Tommy Steele. Dispute was aired as to whether *The Six-Five Special* made Tommy Steele or the other way around. They likely helped each other for the programme raced ahead. At one time it was alleged to have pulled in regular audiences of twelve million people, in a slot that only a short time before had held no programming at all. It was reckoned to be the fastest star-maker and quickest fashion-setter of its time.

Jo Douglas not only co-produced but co-presented with Pete Murray. Freddie Mills, the ex-champion boxer, was in as the funny man. Don Lang and his Frantic Five opened the show with its signature tune. Mike and Bernie Winters were the regular comics and a procession of rock singers was found for the programme. Marty Wilde, Terry Dene, Jackie Dennis, Little Laurie London and the shock-headed Wee Willie Harris all hit the public for the first time on the *Six-Five.* Together with all the dancing youngsters in the studio – which *Top of the Pops* was to emulate a few years later – Jack Good was a happy man tucked up in his control gallery at the Riverside Studios.

A couple of notes from the *Valentine Annual of 1959* read as follows.

A girl named Rosemary Squires had her nose straightened by a little surgical operation, went on *The Six-Five* and whoosh—she was on her way to the top.

A talented young comedian-dancer Jim Dale came on the show and finished up as its regular compere and, to his slight surprise, found himself a rock 'n' roll star.

Malcolm's enjoyment and exhilaration at being on the show could not last long for within a month there was other work to think about and to return him to the fold of the double act. On Monday 10 June Earle & Vaughan began a 17-week summer season starring at the West Cliff Theatre, Clacton. Malcolm and Gaye had been in the east coast resort on their wedding night; now they were to spend their first anniversary in the same town.

It was during the Clacton season and with an addition to the Vaughan family imminent that the double act hit on a particular routine that added to their successful repertoire. In what the pair called their Baby Spot they were dressed up as babies, Earle sitting in an old wheelbarrow and Vaughan in a posh perambulator. The idea was to score points and argue with each other. Malcolm was placed in an example of the brand-named Alwyn Pram. The make was clearly emphasised to the extent that Malcolm in his baby role referred to it as such.

The pram was used later in the year when Gaye's first baby arrived. It was then handed down to her sister-in-law when she too gave birth. Several years beyond that the same Alwyn pram housed the second addition to the Malcolm Vaughan household.

In the 1957 Clacton show, therefore, was possibly one of the first examples of Product Placement, decades before the term was thought of.

There continued to be various dashes back to London for further Sunday night appearances for Malcolm on the *Jack Jackson Show*. The most significant dash, however, took place on another Sunday, with perfect timing on Gaye's part.

Malcolm's entry in his diary for Sunday 22 September reads as follows.

> Our first-born son, born at Guy's Hospital, London Bridge around 1 a.m.-ish. Daryl Earle Haydn Samuel.

Their lives have evinced a number of coincidences, but there is one that Gaye and Malcolm continue to marvel at. A few months before the birth, one of the music papers offered the following note.

If it's a girl, will he and his wife call her Therese? After all 'St Therese of the Roses' is Malcolm's half million seller hit disc.

It clearly was not a girl, but a new-born girl somewhere was given the name because of the record.

Some forty-five years later, Gaye and Malcolm Vaughan moved to Eastbourne. They made the effort of incomers to become involved in their new environment. They joined the Friends of the Devonshire Park Theatre. In so doing they made contact with the membership secretary, Mrs Teresa Nicholson who disclosed to them that her parents had named her after Malcolm's major record success.

14

DOMESTICITY WITH STARDOM

Nappies and sleepless nights became as significant as the trips to Abbey Road, St John's Wood to record new songs, as well as dropping in on the odd television studio to broadcast more comedy with Kenneth Earle, to say nothing of the continuing touring dates. In the midst of all of which, a call to participate in the Royal Variety Performance might well have been little more than an added extra. That it was nothing of the kind was signified by Gaye's allowing seven week-old Daryl to be left for the evening in the care of baby-sitters for the first of only the rarest of times. The baby-sitters were her own parents which took away much of her apprehension. She donned a long gown and joined forces with Mrs Denis Lotis and Mrs Dickie Valentine. The three ladies took their seats in the dress circle of the London Palladium.

The Royal Variety Performance was eagerly awaited more than most as it was the first for two years. In 1956 it had been scheduled for a Monday in November as usual. The artists assembled over the weekend and went through their moves. They gathered for the dress rehearsal at the Palladium on the Monday afternoon. Then a bombshell hit them. The country was at the height of the Suez crisis, when Prime Minister Sir Anthony Eden had sent forces to Egypt following President Nasser's nationalisation of the Suez Canal. The decision was taken at midday that the situation was so serious it was not appropriate for the Queen to attend a variety show. Val Parnell had to tell the company that the show was off. The artist scheduled to fill the star spot before the finale was inconsolable. It would have been the first appearance at a Royal Command by Liberace. He was not to know that several further opportunities would come his way in the ensuing years.

The collective breath was therefore held that nothing would go wrong with the 1957 Royal Performance, incidentally the last to be called a 'Command'. Nor did it. Taking the final spot on the show, Mario Lanza made what was to be one of his last appearances in Britain.

l to r: Denis Lotis, Dickie Valentine, Malcolm Vaughan, Ronnie Hilton, Teddy Johnson, Frankie Vaughan, David Whitfield with Herschel Henlere at the piano in the Royal Variety Performance *of 1957*

The Royal gave Malcolm the opportunity to exercise a burgeoning interest as a cine-enthusiast. He filmed the show on his 16mm camera.

Gaye Vaughan received many cards congratulating her on Daryl's birth but at the party held at the Colony Restaurant after the show, she was enchanted to be approached by Max Bygraves offering his especial good wishes.

In the *Daily Mirror* report and picture showing the Vaughans at the Palladium in their finery, it was noted that Malcolm had just made a new disc entitled 'My Special Angel'.

The record was destined to seal the singing credentials of Malcolm Vaughan. Two weeks after the Royal Variety Performance, on 29 November 1957, it entered the charts and stayed for fourteen weeks. It equalled the highest position reached by Malcolm's recording of 'St Therese' by rising to number three. A pleasing coincidence attached to the record in that the B side was another lilting melody, 'The Heart of a Child'. Its composer was Michael Austin, Malcolm's first professional partner and colleague going back to wartime days with Hal Monty.

As always there was no time to lose and Malcolm had to wrench himself away from family life to honour a commitment in Wolverhampton. The pantomime at the Grand Theatre for Christmas 1957 was *Babes in the Wood* in which Earle and Vaughan played the Robbers for Derek Salberg's production.

Why doesn't Malcolm go solo? By the beginning of 1958 the question was asked even more now that he was being offered twice the amount of money to go it alone as a pop singer than he was receiving as part of a double act. Malcolm had always maintained he had found fame only upon teaming up with Kenneth Earle. In an interview given for *Weekend* in May 1958, Malcolm expressed no regrets for deciding to stick with his partner. He was certain that in comedy there was a more secure future for himself, his wife and his son.

'Singers come and go overnight,' he told Winifred Munday. 'I don't know how long the disc craze will last. I've made quite a lot of money out of my hits and I'm grateful, but people of all ages will always want to laugh.

'I sang around the halls for ten years and sometimes scarcely made enough to eat. I tried to get recording contracts but no one wanted to know me. As soon as Ken and I teamed up, everyone seemed to notice I had a voice. I'm happier working with Ken than I would be on my own.'

Malcolm Vaughan was showing a shrewd sense of foresight. He had seen it happen before. In the *New Musical Express Annual* three years earlier he had observed how John McCormack and other singers of his calibre had been all the rage. The time had come when they no longer were. All singers would become to a greater or lesser degree a lost voice. Malcolm seemed to show at an early age a mature prescience not noted in the world of the popular singer.

Rehearsal for an appearance on the Jack Jackson Show

There was no sign yet, however, of work diminishing. On the contrary, the years 1958 and 1959 were the busiest and most varied in Malcolm Vaughan's career. Nineteen television appearances alone can be traced including seven on the *Jack Jackson Show.* Two further appearances on *The Six-Five Special* involved one of them being broadcast on the Eurovision network, for which Malcolm received an extra £26.5.0d. *The Six-Five* was by then produced by Russell Turner, a sometime son-in-law of Bebe Daniels and Ben Lyon. For ATV there were spots on *Music Shop* and *Lunch Box*; *Top Numbers* for ABC and *Drumbeat* for the BBC. The latter was the follow-up to *The Six-Five Special* when it was decided that the innovative programme had run its course. When Malcolm appeared on *Drumbeat* on Saturday 2 May 1959, a fellow performer was attempting to keep it dark from his day job employer that he was trying his luck not only that evening but on several Saturday nights on the same show. The employer happened to be Aida Young, in charge of a film-editing department at Elstree in days before she became a film producer. When her small daughter raved about the new singer, thereby drawing his performance to Mrs Young's attention, the game was up for Terry Nelhams, who had just changed his name to Adam Faith.

No.................................

ASSOCIATED TELEVISION LIMITED

Television House, Kingsway, London, W.C.2.   *Telephone:* Chancery 4488

REMITTANCE ADVICE

Name Malcolm Vaughan   *Date* 2 APR 1959 ....195......

The attached cheque is in payment of services rendered as follows:—

Programme Title ......Lunch Box......

Transmission Date ......Sun 22. 3. 59

		£	s.	d.
Rehearsal Fees				
Performance Fees		10	10	—
Expenses:				
		10	10	—
Deductions:	Nat. Insurance		9	11
	£	10	=	1

Prepared by ......W. F. Collins....

AC094/1158—36—BE

15

HALCYON YEARS

The record releases continued with 'To Be Loved' on 21 March 1958. Coupled with 'My Loving Arms', it stayed in the charts for twelve weeks, eventually reaching number fourteen. Malcolm was well satisfied that his version sold more copies than the American recording by Jackie Wilson.

Perhaps because of the close resemblance of his first hit record title three years earlier, 'Ev'ry Hour Ev'ry Day of My Life', also released in 1958, did not go anywhere. It was paired with 'Miss You'. The record studios nevertheless continued to keep Malcolm busy with preparations for several EPs (Extended Players) covering three or four songs on each side of the vinyl. One of the EPs was called 'Sincerity in Song' followed by two further volumes under the same title.

It was a good time for a young singer and entertainer. Much has been written in dismissal of the 1950s, usually by people who are not old enough to have been around at the time. It is most often characterised as a decade of dreariness. This was the same decade in which a record number of television sets was bought, altering the face of home entertainment. More refrigerators were purchased, easing the problem of keeping the rest of the Sunday joint in reasonable shape to be had cold with chips during the week. The pressure started to be eased especially for women, often elderly before their time without benefit of labour-saving devices such as a washing machine replacing the old copper in the scullery. More clothes were being bought, and more holidays taken, with seaside resorts around the British coast swarming with fortnightly holidaymakers. Prime Minister Harold Macmillan observed that people 'had never had it so good'. Even many of his detractors did not argue. A future Labour Foreign Secretary, Antony Crosland, was to say years later that he was not surprised the Conservatives had won the 1959 General Election for most people had seen their living standards increase by 20% in the eight years from 1951.

For certain minorities it was still an uneasy time, not to say unjust, but for the overwhelming majority there was a sense of structure, confidence, relaxation to go about personal business without threat of physical violence or verbal abuse. Foul language was not tolerated in public, even less considered to have a part to play in any comedy branches of the entertainment scene. In the Fifties, the most courteous decade of the entire second half of the twentieth century, a sense of order prevailed. Half a century later the positions of the majority and the minorities have been reversed.

In the resulting buoyant atmosphere of the late 1950s, unemployment was almost non-existent. With security of tenure in work, young single people in particular had money to spend, and they made use of the advantage as never before. Dancing lessons, then putting same to good purpose on dance dates at the still operating venues often called the *Palais de Dance,* holidays at the crowded Hi-de-hi camps, variety shows and 'the Pictures' all took care of a sizeable proportion of earned income. And so did the popularity of single '78' records and the fast approaching smaller '45's' – both numbers relating to the rate of revolutions per minute of the respective discs.

In common with his peers Malcolm Vaughan was able to benefit from such a vibrant, disposable income-spending time in the last years of the 1950s. One such advantage was to get away from apartment life, for the young Vaughan family made a move to their first house, in Hoadly Road, Streatham. They bought it from music composer and arranger, Johnny Douglas. Daryl was nearly a year old and had a garden in which to crawl around. Because of the move, in July 1958, Malcolm took a back seat from the hectic business of summer season. With recording and television studios to keep happy, he was nonetheless well occupied.

He made up for lost time on the summer season front the following year with a twelve-week run at the Britannia Pier, Great Yarmouth in company with Kenneth Earle. On his own came Sunday night concerts at Portsmouth, Clacton and the Isle of Wight.

Music hall was not entirely defunct and there were various variety weeks at Cardiff, Manchester Hippodrome, Chiswick Empire (with old chum Alma Cogan), Leeds, Edinburgh and Finsbury Park.

As the variety halls were beginning to be superseded by rock concerts, Malcolm cashed in on the scene. The seeds had been sown with the Bill Haley tour of 1957. As an example Earle & Vaughan spent one week in April 1959 on a tour headed by Marty Wilde, taking them on nightly dates to Pontefract, York, Burnley, Worksop, Wombwell, Nottingham, Newark and Scunthorpe. A cryptic entry appears in Malcolm's diary on the first night of the tour, Sunday 12 April. It is a simple note: 'Oh dear'. Malcolm cannot recall if the comment referred to the entire tour or merely to the town they appeared in that night – which for our purposes shall remain nameless. The fee must have been a compensation for it was a lucrative week. Earle & Vaughan shared the proceeds of £400.

There had been no split of the fee the week before when Malcolm had taken part in a special from the Royal Albert Hall. Presented on the BBC Light Programme – the forerunner to Radio 2 – the Festival of Dance Music was produced by Johnnie Stewart and Geoffrey Owen. Malcolm's diary note shows a fee of £42.5.0d, less the Grade Organisation's commission of £4.4.6d.

The Christmas seasons of 1958 and '59 saw no pantomime work, in the first case largely because Malcolm was booked into the Abbey Road studios from Monday 5 January 1959 to start several weeks preparation for Long Playing records (LPs), or albums as they were eventually called. Instead, Earle & Vaughan spent a week from Boxing Day in variety at Sunderland Empire. The following Christmas found the pair on tour in Germany as support to the popular American group The Platters, from 30 November until New Year's Eve. Malcolm was therefore able to meet up with the team whose recording of 'Only You And You Alone' had, unlike his own cover version three years earlier, been a sensational hit.

In the midst of so much activity and success came a disappointment. Malcolm was earmarked to sing the theme of a prestigious film, *A Night To Remember* which was being prepared at Pinewood in the early spring of 1958. The Rank Organisation planned their production to be a highlight of the cinematic year. To date it is arguably the best of all the many films recounting the Titanic disaster. The producer was William MacQuitty who as a boy had seen the ship under construction in Belfast. The director was a leading one of the day, Roy Ward Baker. The screenplay was adapted from Walter Lord's book of the same name and the central character for the film's story line was the ship's Second Officer Charles Lightoller. Taking the role was one of Britain's top half dozen film stars, Kenneth More. Following his comedy role as Ambrose in *Genevieve* and the more demanding role of Group Captain Douglas Bader in *Reach For The Sky,* More was at the peak of his career.

During the course of the making of the film, a ballad was composed to run across the credits and Malcolm Vaughan was assigned for it. Then it fell through for reasons Malcolm no longer recalls but Gaye Vaughan remembers it as one of very rare occasions when Wally Ridley of HMV let Malcolm down. It was an assignment that was built up to accomplish the kind of prestige for Malcolm's career that the themes of *Born Free* and *Goldfinger* would do for Matt Monro and Shirley Bassey several years later. It was not to be. And what happened to the song entitled 'A Night to Remember'? Three months after the premiere of the film, which grossed bundles for the Rank Organisation, the song appeared as the B side of Malcolm's last big hit, 'More Than Ever', released on 17 October 1958.

Instead of turning another career corner for Malcolm, and a potentially significant one at that, the whole affair appeared to herald, literally, the ides of March. For on a notoriously superstitious day, Friday the thirteenth of March, 1959, another record was released. It was entitled 'Wait For Me', coupled with 'Willingly'. It reached no more than the number of the date of release – thirteen. After that, no further Malcolm Vaughan records reached the charts.

The music recording success therefore ended as quickly as it had begun. Malcolm's anticipation, aided by recollection of what had happened to the likes of John McCormack, proved well-founded.

It was by no means the end of the story. The hit records might have been lost but the voice was not. Malcolm Vaughan was to continue entertaining audiences for another two decades.

16

THE ROAD TO SLOG

The records kept coming, despite not going into the charts. For release in the Christmas season 1959, Malcolm Vaughan made what is still regarded as a beautiful recording of 'You'll Never Walk Alone' before it became the football anthem at the Kop, emphasised by the version of Gerry and the Pacemakers in the early 60s. That was to be at the height of Beatlemania and the Liverpool sound that would take the world by storm. The B side of Malcolm's Christmas record was 'The Holy City', which, given the Vaughan treatment, was also regarded highly.

1960 was the mixture as before. Radio, television, the halls, Abbey Road, summer season, pantomime. Following the release of 'Oh So Wunderbar' coupled with 'For Everyone in Love' on 18 January, Malcolm Vaughan geared himself up to participate in the song festival that has since grown into a massive unwieldy joke of an extravaganza. Most people insist on avoiding it and then do not, if only to listen to Terry Wogan's sending-up of the entire enterprise.

The Eurovision Song Contest first saw the light of day in 1956 in Lugarno, Switzerland. There are some who will vow that it is that competition for which we have to thank for the rise of the European Union, for good or ill depending upon the respective point of view. In fact discussions were already in full swing in Messina between the original six nations intent on creating a federal body in Europe. The discussions led to the Treaty of Rome, signed in March 1957 which set up the European Common Market. The United Kingdom was not one of the Six.

There was a time when Britain's entry in the Eurovision Song Contest involved only one singer who showcased all six entries in a British knockout. The public were invited to telephone their vote and the winning song with the same singer went forward to the event itself, usually hosted by the country who had won the previous year's contest.

In recent years *A Song For Europe* has reverted to the format of its early days when each entry was sung by a different performer. In the fourth year of the contest Malcolm Vaughan was chosen to sing one of the songs and he duly arrived at the Television Theatre, Shepherd's Bush at 11 o'clock on the morning of Monday 2 February 1960. The host for the programme to go out live that night at 9.15pm was David Jacobs whom Malcolm recalls meeting and liking greatly. The BBC contract allowed for a fee of fifty-five guineas (£57.75p) together with the following stipulation.

It is agreed that the Corporation shall have an option on the same terms and conditions on your services for two further programmes on 6 February and 29 March, with rehearsal on 28 March should your song win through to the British Finals and the European Finals.

Malcolm's song, 'Each Tomorrow', won through to the second round so that he appeared again on the following Saturday evening in heightened atmosphere, the programme produced by Harry Carlisle.

The secretary of Malcolm's fan club of the time, Maureen Gladman, recalls sitting next to Kenneth Earle in the Television Theatre, the two of them cheering him on. But it proved to be the end of the road with Malcolm finishing in fourth position. The song that went forward to compete in the Eurovision Song Contest the following month was 'Looking High High High', sung by Bryan Johnson. Britain was the host and the event at the Royal Festival Hall was compered by Catherine (Katie) Boyle. Bryan Johnson was pipped at the post by the French entry, 'Tom Pilibi' sung by Jacqueline Boyer.

Gaye Vaughan has a vivid memory of their treasured home help, Doris, who vowed that David Hughes, who had come second in the British finals with 'Mi Amor' beat Malcolm only because Welsh viewers had voted in droves for him. Doris had no idea that Malcolm had come from the same principality and Gaye did not like to disabuse her of the notion.

The vicissitudes of show business ensured that Malcolm Vaughan came down to earth with a bump following the comparative glamour of Eurovision. *Workers' Playtime* was a radio show on the BBC Light Programme left over from the War which still survived into peace time. It went out daily at 12.30 and was broadcast live from works' canteens situated in various parts of the country. On St David's Day, Monday 1 March, Malcolm found himself entertaining the workforce of British Resin Products Limited, Penarth, Glamorgan.

The following week saw another disc released: 'My Love For You' coupled with 'Lady of Spain'. On the night of the release, 11 March, Malcolm was back in Wales for *Spotlight,* a BBC television show from Cardiff. An up-and-coming young actor caught Malcolm's eye on the show and he has recorded the brief note in his diary. 'It was on this TV programme that I first met and enjoyed the company of Victor Spinetti.'

Trumpeter Kenny Baker was described in the same journal as a 'fabulous guy' arising from a ten-day tour of USAF camps in Germany in April.

Six months of summer season in the Channel Islands immediately followed by six weeks on the Moss Empire circuit brought Malcolm up to pantomime rehearsals and a meeting with an artist who became a lifelong friend to both Mal and Gaye. Appearing in *Mother Goose* at Bolton was Dave Allen. Another brief note in Malcolm's diary states simply: 'First meeting with our pal.'

They maintained a friendship to the extent that after their move to Eastbourne they travelled to London in 2005 to Dave and Karin Allen's Kensington home where they stayed overnight. They observed that the comedian was looking off colour but had no idea how ill he was. Indeed Gaye Vaughan notes: 'During the evening, especially whilst chatting over dinner, signs of the old Dave emerged – the marvellous sense of humour and the twinkle in his eyes.'

They were not to know that Dave Allen had but a fortnight to live.

Gaye further recalls his penchant for practical jokes. 'If Dave took a photograph, he would spend an age posing the subjects, asking them to stand this way and that so that they would remember the occasion. When the picture was developed, all you would see were the feet.'

The billing for *Mother Goose* has a very 1960 look about it: Hylda Baker, Dave Allen, Earle & Vaughan and The Mudlarks. Miss Baker was still basking in her new-found film success, having just co-starred with Albert Finney in the ground-breaking *Saturday Night And Sunday Morning*.

Early in the New Year came the first of two long seasons in Australia, arranged by Jack Neary who was a former policeman turned theatre promoter. Earle & Vaughan played the Menzies Hotel in Sydney, named after the former prime minister Sir Robert Menzies. They met among others Kerry Packer and a young Rupert Murdoch. They appeared on television and played various night clubs and travelled to Melbourne.

A similar trip took place three years later. During the eight-week season that began in March 1964, they not only played Melbourne and travelled across to the Western Australian capital, Perth, but the trip was memorable in two particular ways.

First they opened the Chequers Night Club, Sydney. It was heralded as a prestigious venue and a considerable honour for Earle & Vaughan who shared the top billing with the popular American crooner of the time, Dick Haymes. They were followed three weeks after the opening by Shirley Bassey.

Dealing with Mr Haymes could be difficult. Malcolm recalled several years later that although they found him a 'nice, quiet man', he tended to hit the bottle, often unexpectedly.

'We compered the whole show and introduced Haymes. His manager always stood in the wings. He told us if he held his hand up and waved it from right to left, it meant Dick wouldn't be coming on. It never reached that stage except for one night when it nearly did. But they managed to get him on.'

The pair also took part in launching the new television station, Channel Seven. In the opening-night programme with them were the British comedian Jimmy Edwards and the American show band man Bob Crosby, brother of Bing. Resources were so limited on the new channel that Kenneth Earle remembers ventriloquist Dennis Spicer being signalled to stop during his act. The reason for a floor manager 'turning the handle' at him was that they needed the camera that was trained on him to broadcast the next news bulletin.

The equivalent of the Royal British Legion in Australia was the Returned Servicemen's League. Their venues were on a far more lavish scale with gambling machines reminiscent of Las Vegas. The pair were booked for as many of the clubs as they could fit in during the time.

That was not easy, for Earle & Vaughan had their own television series of six programmes on the already existing Channel Five. So successful was it that they were tried out in a pilot for another series. For Malcolm the call of home was too strong and he said he did not want to prolong the stay.

On which note Gaye Vaughan recalls vividly how she never heard what the different places were like.

'He was such a home bird that none of his letters contained news of what was happening and what was seen. It was all enquires about me and the boys.'

For indeed the family had grown by then. Damon Vaughan was born on 12 February 1963, which event completed the Vaughan family unit.

Malcolm's decision was clearly influenced by the amount of time he was spending abroad in general. In the autumn of 1962 had come a tour for Combined Services Entertainment to Malta, Cyprus and North Africa.

Reminded of entertaining troops in faraway places, Kenneth Earle's distinct memory of a hair-raising experience in Borneo resurfaced in conversation with Gaye Vaughan.

Following the troubles in Malaya, the Federation of Malaysia was created. Indonesia objected to it and mounted armed opposition. Their campaign began in April 1963 with regular incursions into Borneo. Major General Walker, Commander, British Forces, Borneo, was faced with defending a border 900 miles long, mostly in heavy jungle. He established fortified posts along the border as bases for patrols and sites for field artillery. Walker provided support for infantry units on patrol. Helicopters played a significant role in maintaining the outposts.

Towards the end of 1963 the situation was stabilised though it was to remain in stalemate until the Indonesian leader, Achmed Sukarno, was deposed by General Suharto in March 1966.

During one of the crucial months in the early stages of the conflict, Earle & Vaughan were booked to entertain the troops in Borneo. The trip was organised by Derek Agutter, father of Jenny. The intrepid pair went from camp to camp.

No place names were mentioned. Locations were given such descriptions as Hill 203. At one such reference where they had performed, they later discovered that it had been 'wiped out'. Their stage might have been a vast concrete slab, a gunsight or the back of a lorry. Wherever it was, they always wore dinner jackets. It was on one of these occasions that Earle & Vaughan had to stop in mid-performance because insurgents started firing at them. They were forced to escape by helicopter.

To the best of their knowledge the gunfire attack on them was not a response to their act.

17

MISS DORS AND DOUBLE EGG 'N' CHIPS

December 1964 found Earle & Vaughan in pantomime at the New Theatre, Bromley. By then the 'New' was rather old and decrepit. It was to be demolished about ten years later and replaced by the Churchill Theatre, albeit further along the road. The pantomime was *Sleeping Beauty*. Playing the Prince was Diana Dors.

Miss Dors was in a trough in her career. She would rise again to the heights in the early 70s on starring with Jill Bennett in *Three Months Gone* at the Duchess Theatre, London, a play that was not only to revive her career but give her the chance to show her true capabilities as an actress. Throughout her film work she had not been granted a realistic rating, even following her remarkable performance as the condemned woman, Mary Hilton, in *Yield To The Night*. That part had come in the middle of her blonde bombshell days and had run counter to her usual roles. Her due recognition was still to come.

By 1964 Diana Dors had not long returned from Hollywood where she had gained mixed fortunes. Film roles had come along including that of *I Married A Woman,* co-starring the American comedian George Gobel. She had won a stronger role in the form of *The Unholy Wife* in company with Rod Steiger. There was a Danny Kaye comedy that had included Margaret Rutherford and which had awarded her the separate billing 'and Miss Diana Dors'. Television variety shows of the period also gave her a platform, including one starring Phil Silvers and Sydney Chaplin.

She returned to England in the early 60s and made a couple of British films, notably *West Eleven* directed by Michael Winner, a gritty tale of Notting Hill life with Alfred Lynch and Kathleen Breck. She was at a low ebb professionally but always went looking for work. Her friend, the late Andrew Ray, described her as 'a grafter'.

In that frame Diana Dors fetched up at Bromley to play the Prince. The local paper liked her performance but declared there was not enough of it. She arrived not before the second half and did not have to accomplish much after that.

Diana Dors was also at a low ebb personally. Her marriage to British comedian Dickie Dawson had folded while they were in America. Dawson's career appeared to flourish more in California so he did not want to leave. It was decided that the two young boys who had been born to Dors would fare better in the States so she came back empty-handed of family. She took on a succession of boy friends, most of whom were 'unreliable', including the 1964 one in tow. Troy Dante has confessed to the description of himself on television in subsequent years and he it was who was given a role in the pantomime.

Gaye Vaughan recalls vividly Diana's reaction to her own boys who were about the same age as Dors' own. In Gaye's words: 'She was all over them.' Gaye and Malcolm were still living at the house in Hoadly Road, Streatham, a short distance from Bromley, and Gaye recalls that Diana liked nothing better than going back with them after a show for a plate of egg and chips.

When it came to Christmas, Gaye wondered what could be bought for someone like Diana Dors. She remembered that the star had a fondness for pickled onions. She took a chance, bought a large jar, wrapped it suitably in festive paper and offered it up. Apparently Dors was thrilled to have the gift.

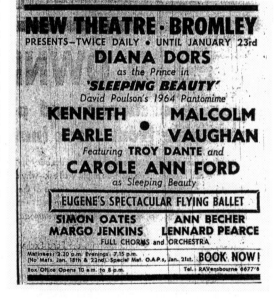

Christmas 1964

Both Malcolm and Gaye recall Diana Dors with fondness. Gaye says she was a person with whom you knew where you stood. She could be outrageous and never apologised for herself. That made in Gaye's view for a consistent personality. She and Malcolm were invited to several parties at Dors' Chelsea flat. The point in the evening would be reached where, in Gaye's words, 'silly games' would start such as Truth or Consequences with couples disappearing into a bedroom. At such a point Mal and Gaye would nod at each other, collect their coats and quietly leave. Nothing would be said the next time they saw Diana and Gaye was always glad that Dors for her part would never make an apology.

Their friendship was to last a number of years. Earle & Vaughan played the Playboy Club in Park Lane for two consecutive years, scoring a massive hit on both occasions. Diana Dors went to their first appearance in 1968. Malcolm and the whole family returned the compliment several years later when Diana played the Country Cousin in Chelsea, having taken up cabaret work herself.

In November 1968 Diana Dors married for the third time. She had met Alan Lake on a Yorkshire Television series, *Queenie's Castle* which became a success. They would go on to play in *Three Months Gone* together at the Duchess Theatre. Lake was not the most stable of personalities, obtaining for himself a custodial sentence following a brawl. However, the marriage proved to be her most successful and they had a son, Jason.

In the early 1980s Diana Dors contracted cancer and soldiered on with her final film while still suffering. She played the bath attendant in the screen adaptation of Nell Dunn's prestigious play *Steaming,* itself to be the final film directed by Joseph Losey. Shortly after shooting was completed in 1984 Diana Dors died. She was fifty-two. A matter of weeks later, on the day before the Grand Hotel, Brighton was bombed with Prime Minister Margaret Thatcher and most of the Government inside it, Alan Lake ended his own life with a shotgun.

At the Playboy Club in November 1969 the American entertainment journal, *Variety,* said the following about Kenneth Earle and Malcolm Vaughan, making their second appearance there.

Guest spot is in the capable hands of Earle & Vaughan, one of this country's top rib-tickling duos, very fast with the ad lib and keen sensers of audience moods. Not only because this seems to be the day of the Anglo performer in the U.S. after-dark circuit, the pair merit a stateside looksee and, with suitably adapted material, could break out of their now firmly established Blighty niche. Vaughan also has a very pleasing singing voice, which he displays as interludes to the laugh sessions.

In the hit-and-miss world of show business, however, America did not happen. Given Malcolm's philosophical approach to fame and success, and his utmost dedication to his family life, it is doubtful that he would have agreed to any long-term plan involving stardom in the United States, any more than his namesake, Frankie Vaughan, had been persuaded a few years earlier.

18

THE DICK RAY YEARS BEGIN

For many years from 1960 Malcolm Vaughan enjoyed a working relationship with the Channel Islands impresario Dick Ray, whose entire life was steeped in show business. Which could scarcely have been avoided. For example, his uncle was Herbert Ray, a producer from the 1920s. In 1928 Herbert put out a tour of the revue *HMV* featuring among others the soubrette Freda Gardner, the same Freda who eventually married George Bolton. Until her death shortly before publication she was living in a retirement home close to Eastbourne's sea front, having reached her one hundredth birthday. Freda recalled playing opposite one, Bill Sellers, brother-in-law of Herbert Ray, which made Dick Ray first cousin to Bill's son, Peter Sellers.

Dick Ray moved to Jersey in 1957 and concentrated much of his production work in the Channel Islands, putting on shows at the Opera House, St Helier which he eventually bought. One of his several other venues, and one that featured most notably in Malcolm Vaughan's life, was the Watersplash dinner show venue. It was situated approximately in the middle of La Grande Route Des Mielles, usually referred to as Five Mile Road covering the same distance of beach along St Ouen's Bay on the western coast of the island. There was little else for miles either side of the venue so that audience members took a pleasant evening drive on summer evenings to have dinner and see the show.

On Saturday 7 May 1960, the day after Princess Margaret married Anthony Armstrong Jones, Earle & Vaughan first took to the stage of the Watersplash for a total of twenty-two weeks in Dick Ray's show revue then in its third year under the general title *Excitement*, always accompanied by a subtitle. In this case it was *Deadwood Stage*. The show was an enormous success and the delighted owner of the Watersplash, Harry Swanson, invested in two pairs of prize cufflinks for the show's stars. Kenneth Earle has his to this day but Malcolm's were taken in a house burglary years later.

In April the following year, the day after appearing on television in *The Charlie Chester Show*, the pair left again for the Watersplash and another long successful summer season. Patrons would arrive early for dinner and at 8.45 the show started, going on often until well after 11 o'clock.

Appearing at the Swanson's Music Hall in the summer of 1961 were Mike and Bernie Winters and Frank Ifield. At the Opera House were Jon Pertwee, Dave Allen and a double act, the Konyots. Forty-five years later, Gaye and Malcolm Vaughan attended a theatre awards lunch organised by the entertainment trade magazine, *Encore*, and found themselves sitting down opposite Marion Konyot. They had not seen each other in the interim. The reunion of the Vaughans with Dave Allen in the summer of 1961 cemented the friendship begun at the Bolton pantomime the previous Christmas. They shared a bungalow in the St Saviour district of Jersey and Dave Allen's accommodation was in the attic. Access was via a step ladder pulled down from the loft. According to Gaye, Dave would climb it every night accompanying the exercise with an impression of Quasimodo from *The Hunchback of Notre Dame.*

The Vaughans' summer accommodation St Saviour, Jersey, 1961.
Dave Allen slept in the loft.

During the many years when summer seasons thrived in seaside towns with several theatres each, the companies would get together frequently, joining forces for midnight matinees, usually for a selected charity, or for weekend garden fetes and town shows. Or they would team up for beach trips to enjoy the company of old friends who had often worked together elsewhere. And it provided the ideal situation where newer friendships were forged, as in the case of Malcolm Vaughan and Dave Allen, who in all the following years of keeping in touch in fact never worked together again in 'the business'.

On one of the Saturday afternoon outdoor functions in Jersey, the artists were invited to participate in various sporting activities. Malcolm took part in a go-karting race and succeeded in beating Jon Pertwee to the finishing line. Pertwee could never take defeat lightly in anything. His action, therefore, of pouring champagne over Malcolm's head was not entirely in jest. But it did provide the *Jersey Evening Post* with a first-rate photo which showed another cast member of the Watersplash show only just avoiding the cascade. She was a name from the British movie days of the 1950s. Vera Day had first come to prominence playing the daughter of Jack Warner and Kathleen Harrison in the radio series, *Meet The Huggetts* in which she had taken over the part following the untimely death of Joan Dowling. Vera had gone on to feature in the acclaimed 1955 Carol Reed film, *A Kid For Two Farthings.*

For the second consecutive year the summer season was followed by an autumn programme for Bernard Delfont in the now dwindling Moss Empire variety circuit: Bristol, Liverpool, Manchester and so on. The combined fee for Earle & Vaughan was £200 per week to be split between the two. A clause was still being stipulated in the Delfont contract.

> It is agreed and understood that the Artistes will not televise during this engagement without the mutual consent of the Management.

During the year another two Malcolm Vaughan record releases coupled 'There's No Other Love' with 'La Dolce Vita' and 'The Wedding' with 'Guardian Angel'. Malcolm reflected several years later on how one of the titles was expected to be a success but failed to make its mark.

'We did "The Wedding" first and it was never a hit. I think the trouble was that it was not considered a male song, and of course it did become a very big hit for Julie Rogers.'

'Guardian Angel' was deployed for the second time as the B side. The first occasion had been four years earlier when it had accompanied 'Chapel of the Roses'.

1962 found Earle & Vaughan taking a break from the Channel Islands and their summer was spent at the Grand Pavilion, Bridlington. Malcolm was able to indulge in his growing passion for golf and reported in a letter to an old family friend, Kevin Lewis, that he had become a member of the Vaudeville Golfing Society, advising that Ted Ray had 'pushed him through'. In the same letter dated 22 August Malcolm pointed out that he and Kenneth Earle had unexpectedly moved up to star billing, displacing an old north country comedian of the time.

> I don't know whether you know, Kev, but Ted Lune left the show about four weeks ago and Ken and I took over the starring as it were. I am pleased to say the figures have gone up for us but I believe it's been a bad summer all over the country. You will be pleased to know that I am going to be a daddy again in February which is pretty wonderful and as you can imagine we are thrilled to bits. We have had a hard summer from the point of view of graft. Ken and I have been working every Sunday since we got here so we feel a bit bushed. We have three weeks to go up here and then home sweet home – for only three days! Ken and I then leave for Malta, Cyprus and North Africa which will be sunny I hope. Well, mate, it will soon be time to go to the fun factory so I must end this letter.

At the end of the year came Malcolm's final single record release for HMV which paired 'This Side of Heaven' with 'The Love of a Lifetime'. A significant phase in Malcolm Vaughan's career thus drew to a close. It had been seven years earlier that he had first stepped into the recording studio. It was time for other singers and other styles to take his place at Abbey Road.

19

MORE ROADS TO THE ISLES

Back to the Channel Islands the following year though not to Jersey. From 3 June to 21 September Earle & Vaughan featured in Dick Ray's *A Night in Las Vegas* at the Hermitage Starlight Room, Guernsey. It told of one hundred years in the playground city of Nevada starting with the Silver Dollar Saloon in 1863 and featuring singer Dick Powell – not to be confused with the veteran Hollywood star – and six dancing ladies including Marlene Foster.

Dick Ray often centred his shows around a specific theme rather than adopt the fading variety bill format involving one turn after another. One example was his 1965 show at the Watersplash, sub-titled: *Earle & Vaughan at The Olympics*. The world sports competition had recently taken place in Tokyo and was still in people's minds. The first scene of the show therefore featured The First Olympics in the Ancient Greece of 776 BC. The billing told the audience they would see 'The Torch Runner' and then 'Hercules lights the Fire and introduces the Watersplash Singers and Dancers'. The action moved on to London 1948, Helsinki 1952 and Melbourne 1956, providing the opportunity to present a new Decca signing from Australia, Robby Royal. Reg Drew, Vic Abbott and his Orchestra and the Archdale Sisters were all featured as well as 'the Golden Voice of Malcolm Vaughan' when he was not bantering around as part of Earle & Vaughan.

Work in the Channel Islands continued over the years with further engagements at the Watersplash and the Hermitage Hotel, Guernsey all to help pay for the mortgage and a young family.

It was never a straightforward matter renting accommodation in Jersey. Anybody in the business who wished to rent a flat or house in the island had to justify himself with the Housing Committee. He had to explain his purpose in working there. Dick Ray played a crucial role in the procedure by emphasising to the Committee that 'there is no one else to do the job'.

By permission of the Ballet

1965 EDITION
8th YEAR

"Excitement"
at the Watersplash

First performance Easter Saturday
17th April, 1965

THE HOME OF GOOD ENTERTAINMENT

Kenneth Earle *and* Malcolm Vaughan

When the author met Dick Ray and asked him what would happen if he wanted to book Dame Shirley Bassey, the producer reported that he would have to go through the same process.

In 1970 Earle & Vaughan took another break from Dick Ray's productions and were booked in for a summer season at the Palace Hotel, Douglas, Isle of Man. The venue was owned by Sir Dudley Cunliffe-Owen who created the King's Room for entertainment. He organised what were described as Gambling Junkets which for some reason drew in a large clientele from Canada. For Malcolm it proved a different proposition, as he let his feelings be known to Kevin Lewis in a letter on 22 July. The Douglas of forty years ago was clearly not to his liking.

I have as you know been here for 12 weeks now. It's very difficult to describe the island. It's nowhere near as rewarding as Jersey. The countryside I must admit is beautiful and that's about it. The main town of Douglas is awful, they would win the gold medal for Wimpy bars and fish and chip shops. In many ways it's like walking around Coronation Street.

Signs of disillusion were also setting in regarding his work.

This so-called Show Biz of ours is becoming more and more distasteful to me as I go on night after night performing like a puppet, but as we have discussed so often, Kev, it's merely a question of finance isn't it? The older I get it seems that one's commitments in life become more permanent. However, I suppose that's what life's all about. Wasn't it Byron who said: 'If it's not one long struggle, it's not worth living'? Ah well, that's how the cookie crumbles, or words to that effect.

At the moment of writing this bad letter, it's absolutely pouring with rain, and as I am staying in a cottage right in the country it's deathly quiet. Still I must admit I prefer the peace of the rural bit, as opposed to the smells of Douglas.

Malcolm's acerbic stance might have been influenced from the bout of ill-health he was suffering as a result of kidney stones.

The first five weeks of my stay over here were very painful, Kev, as you can imagine. However, the stones aren't troubling me now, but pain is the most demoralising thing as it affects everything one does and changes the normal personality into a very dour one. But enough of my problems, Kev, the thing I am interested in at the moment is news of yourself.

The letter was not all doom and as the season had moved on, Malcolm had been able to indulge his sporting passion.

I have spent every day recently on the golf course and I do enjoy that, and by God, my game has improved so much that the minute I'm home I shall be calling for you and we will see how well we can cope with dear old Mitcham again.

Happy memories that brings back to me; we had some great days there with Des *(Lane)* – remember?

The following summer of 1971 saw Malcolm back in his beloved Jersey and for the second time in their careers Earle & Vaughan found themselves moved up unexpectedly into the star slot. It had happened with Ted Lune's departure from the Bridlington show in 1962 but now a tragic event was to alter the billing. Dick Ray had booked Malcolm's contemporary, and fellow participant in the 1957 Royal Variety Performance, Dickie Valentine, to star in the show at the Watersplash. Everything was in place until Valentine was killed in a car crash one week before the opening. The format was hastily rearranged, giving Earle & Vaughan star billing and featuring a new singer, a resident of Jersey, Stuart Gillies.

Yet if 1971 had proved crucial, the following year at the same venue was to be the most significant so far in the careers of Kenneth Earle and Malcolm Vaughan.

*Above: Jon Pertwee pours champagne over Malcolm while Vera Day escapes. Jersey, 1961.
(Photo: Jersey Evening Post)*

Left: Dave Allen with Daryl, Portelet Bay, Jersey, 1961.

Malcolm, Gaye, Ann Hart, David Watson, Ronnie Corbett, at Danny La Rue's Club, summer, 1964.

The family at Hoadly Road, Streatham prior to leaving for the summer in Jersey, 1965.

Earle & Vaughan appearing at the Showboat, London, 1966.

Sixties fashions for a Sixties wedding. Malcolm and Gaye set off to see Denis King of the King Brothers get married.

*Following Earle &
Vaughan's act at the Playboy
Club, they relax with
audience members including
Diana Dors, Gaye and
Leapy Lee, 1968.*

*Damon, Gaye and Daryl
at the Watersplash, Jersey,
August 1972.*

The Blackpool variety scene, summer, 1973 including Wyn Calvin, Ken Barnes, Reg Swinson, Malcolm, Eric Coverdale, Clinton Ford, Peter Webster, Danny La Rue, Ben Warriss.

Those Good Old Days, *Central Pier, Blackpool, 1973 – Wyn Calvin, Christine Cartwright, Anna da Costa, Malcolm.*

Gaye, Damon and Malcolm with Diana Dors at the Country Cousin, Chelsea, 1973.

20th wedding anniversary, Jersey, June, 1976.

Gaye and Damon, Jersey, 1976.

Daryl and Malcolm, Jersey, 1976.

20

A PARTNERSHIP ENDS

The period between 1967 and 1972 saw several major upheavals for the Vaughans, professionally and domestically. The first was the move from Hoadly Road, Streatham after nine years. One reason for it was the devastating car accident that befell their 'treasure', Doris, which rendered her paraplegic. Gaye and Malcolm did not want to stay in the house after that so they sold it to the most willing of buyers, one, Roy Hudd.

Daryl and Damon were ten and four years old respectively and the family moved to Reigate. Gaye now says she knew almost immediately it was a wrong move and they were to stay for less than a year. In May 1968 they bought 'Antares' in the village of Salfords, Surrey for £11,000. There was little summer season work during 1967 so time was taken up on household chores and decoration.

The 1968 summer season took a different form from the usual. It seemed innocuous at the time but would now be classed as illegal. Centred in Norfolk it was entitled unashamedly *The Players No 6 Show*. Sponsored by the tobacco giant it saw the usual variety show format with Earle & Vaughan but with one essential difference. At every opportunity the boys went around the audience offering the customers free cigarettes in an effort to encourage them to choose to smoke more of the Players No 6 brand. The show played at various venues a few days at a time, including the community halls of caravan sites on the Great Yarmouth coast, moving south and including Butlin's Camp, Clacton.

Work of a more conventional nature picked up in the autumn of 1968 with the first of the two dates at the Playboy Club and a three-week season touring South Africa for African Consolidated Theatres. For that they had the company of French singer and heart-throb Johnny Halliday. No sooner had the tour finished than Earle & Vaughan were scheduled to be in Brighton for *Cinderella* at the

Theatre Royal. They co-starred alongside Bernard Bresslaw, Yana, Clive Dunn and George Bolton.

By 1970 the Vaughans had installed Daryl and Damon in Alleyn's School, Dulwich and the travelling was becoming a problem, so they decided to move back closer to old roots. In the May the family moved into 156 Cheviot Road, West Norwood, on the doorstep of the boys' school.

In the spring of 1972 Malcolm took a cruise job. In lieu of pay he decided to take Gaye and they had a holiday out of it on the P & 0 liner 'Chusan' which drifted them leisurely around the Mediterranean. Gaye was still working as Malcolm's secretary, at a rate of £7 per week. They decided more regular pay needed to come into the household kitty and Gaye became a receptionist at a hairdresser's in Streatham where she was paid £18 per week.

Then came the summer season. As with the year before, Earle & Vaughan starred in *The Viva Las Vegas Show* at the Watersplash, Jersey. It was generally regarded as a fun show that again featured singer Stuart Gillies.

One of Stuart's duties towards the end of the show was to introduce a Scottish piper who came on to play 'Amazing Grace'. Each night the piper had to warm up the bagpipes outside the theatre so that they were ready for the performance. The coach drivers conducting their evening tours around the island became used to seeing the sight of the Scottish piper at work. The season progressed and dusk started setting in as they weaved their way around the relevant part of the island back to the hotels. Between them the coach drivers hit on a wheeze for their customers.

Sir Walter Raleigh had been the first Governor General of Jersey. He had come to a sorry end on a chopping block. The drivers devised the story that Raleigh's piper at the time in Jersey had been so distraught at what had happened to his master that the piper's ghost walked abroad nightly on the remoter part of the island where the Watersplash was situated.

'Look carefully,' the drivers would tell their passengers as they passed by, 'and you may well see the ghost of Sir Walter Raleigh's piper.' They timed their approach each night to coincide with the piper's warm-up rehearsal, slowing down their vehicles to five miles per hour. It is not known how many sight-seeing coach customers were taken in.

Dick Ray recalls that one night the piper was left out of the show. Stuart Gillies went on as usual and began taking requests from the audience, as was the procedure. It happened to be pouring with rain. The piper was loath to be cast out into it but was firmly told he could not 'warm up' in earshot of the audience. Stuart took more requests than usual and got carried away, entirely forgetting the piper. The bagpipes were warmed up and the piper was soaked through, to no purpose for he did not get a showing that particular night.

There was also a young dancer in the troupe called Janice Peeling, in her twenties and from Edmonton, north London. She would change her name to Jan Lynton and go on to become a choreographer for many seasons for John Redgrave in the Isle of Wight and at Torquay and Eastbourne.

Daryl and Damon Vaughan spent several weeks with their parents in excellent weather. The atmosphere was convivial and yet again *The Viva Las Vegas Show* did good business. Then a bombshell fell on Kenneth Earle.

Unbeknown to Earle, Malcolm had, for some time, felt they had come to the end of the line in their partnership. Gaye now says that Malcolm was never one for talking things through when ideas first came to him. During the summer of 1972 Malcolm let the idea build and then announced to Kenneth Earle that he wanted to call it a day. It was a shock. After twenty-one weeks in Jersey and following eighteen years, the last performance of Earle & Vaughan took place at the Watersplash on Saturday 12 October 1972.

21

TRANSITION TIME

Something of the difficulty in which Malcolm found himself is
evidenced in a letter to his friend Kevin Lewis dated 8 August
1972. Towards the end of the letter Malcolm wrote:

> Kev, there is not much more news from here. I'm hoping
> that all will be well with me at the end of the season – but
> we will wait and see what's in store.

The letter also provides an insight into Malcolm Vaughan's
detachment from the trappings of show business. It was written at 1.30
in the morning in the house where he was lodged for the summer,
'Annsholme' in the Beaumont district of Jersey. Malcolm reported
that he had just come up from the kitchen having treated himself to
'a midnight snack and cup of tea'.

> The scene over here is very much the same, everything
> going on in its own intriguing way. I am not feeling so
> lonely now that the boys are with me – and I hope Gaye
> will be over real soon as well then it won't be long before
> I'm home again.

Several artists were installed in 'Annsholme' including Jan Lynton.
In recent years she has admitted that she has only really got to know
Malcolm latterly.

'In those days,' she told him in 2007, 'you always left the theatre
immediately after the show to get back to the family.'

Jan Lynton met Gaye and Malcolm again through a coincidence.
A longtime resident of Eastbourne, she was being interviewed on the
local hospital radio service, Radio DGH, appearing on their Friday
night programme, *Showtime*. A fortnight earlier the programme
host, Phil Moon, had persuaded Malcolm Vaughan to come to the
studio for an interview that would be interspersed with his records.

Malcolm and Gaye had themselves moved to Eastbourne a couple of years earlier.

In the course of the programme featuring Jan Lynton she happened to observe that she seemed to be noted for appearing in shows that had seen the last appearances of double acts. She went through the list.

'Jewel and Warriss, Mike and Bernie Winters, Earle and Vaughan.'

Phil Moon immediately picked it up. 'Are you talking about Malcolm Vaughan?'

When she confirmed as much he disclosed to her that Malcolm and his wife were now in Eastbourne. It was further discovered that the two parties had been living around the corner from each other for at least two years. A couple of weeks later, and after thirty years, the Vaughans and Jan Lynton were reunited at a function held at Eastbourne's Winter Garden.

At approximately the same time Malcolm undertook the radio interview with John Hannam for Isle of Wight Radio. Hannam asked Malcolm whether in looking back he had ever wished to reach the top of the comedy ladder so that Earle & Vaughan would have enjoyed the same prestige as Jewel & Warriss or Morecambe & Wise. Malcolm answered with an emphatic negative. Much as he had enjoyed doing comedy, in the last analysis singing had been his first love and more akin to his personal style.

The eighteen-year partnership of Earle & Vaughan had been eventful to say the least. They had known hungry times before they had teamed up and also during the first year before their big break, orchestrated by Jack Jackson in 1955. However, even after they had hit the big time, they had encountered difficult moments, as for example an engagement in Salzburg. Owing to some misunderstanding the pair thought they would be paid immediately following the performance whereas the money was not forthcoming until the end of the week. They had no spare cash. They wandered the streets hungry and asked at a delicatessen if they could be lent some food. They had to leave their passports on account.

Nor had their television experience always been a roaring success. In the early Sixties they had been lined up for a series put out by

Associated Rediffusion. It was called *It Shouldn't Happen to a Dog* and involved the writing talents of such as Terry Nation, of Dr Who fame, and the participation of actor/comedian John Junkin. The pilot was made and crashed to earth. The selector of the title had clearly asked for trouble. Commented one critic: 'No, it *certainly* shouldn't happen to a dog!'

There had also been the occasion when Earle & Vaughan were doing a show in Sligo, Ireland. They had not realized the need to finish their act with the Irish national anthem. The audience had been with them all the way but the oversight had turned them to such a degree of anger that the pair had had to be smuggled out of the venue with blankets thrown over their heads.

Tours of Ireland could be fraught with difficulties. At around the same time Alma Cogan's musical director preceded her to various dates to check the arrangements. At one of the smaller venues he spotted a decrepit upright piano and spoke to the man in charge.

'I'm afraid you will have to get a much better piano than this, a grand piano in fact. Miss Cogan can't possibly be accompanied on this.'

The man assured him all would be well on the night. Came the night and Alma Cogan and her MD arrived to find a different piano installed but it was still an upright. The MD was incensed.

'I asked you specifically to obtain a grand piano,' he ranted.'Oh, but to be sure,' protested the man.'Isn't this one of the grandest pianos you ever saw?'

The 'gofer' on the Irish tour in the early Sixties was Nuggie McGraw.

While Earle & Vaughan were in Dublin he happened to mention that one of Malcolm's screen idols was in town. Malcolm begged Nuggie to arrange a meeting, which he did. By that time Malcolm had met a truckload of stars, yet now, at the appointed time he found he had developed a bout of nerves upon speaking to this famous face and greeted the man with: 'I've always wanted to meet you, Mr Cagney.' The Yankee Doodle Dandy merely said:'Yes, what is it, son?' The two chatted for only a short while before, as Malcolm recalls, two priests came across to interrupt and take James Cagney away.

Any friction between Malcolm Vaughan and Kenneth Earle following the break in October 1972 was not long-lived and the two men remain friends to this day. Kenneth Earle did not continue as a performer, preferring instead to go into the agency side of the business.

Malcolm found himself back exclusively as a solo artist, for the first time since his days as Malcolm Thomas in the early 1950s. Work started pouring in again but of a different nature. Malcolm set out in earnest on the one-nighter circuit. It was to take its toll eventually but for the time being he was content to travel and to receive payment that no longer had to be split two ways as had been the case with his double-act partnership.

On 29 October 1972, two and a half weeks after the split with Kenneth Earle, Malcolm Vaughan resumed his solo career. He appeared in Newcastle although he cannot recall the venue. His fee was £300. For the first time in eighteen years he was able to keep all of it, except for the fee for his musical director. He had acquired the services of Gary Lloyd with whom he had worked a great deal in the Channel Islands. Malcolm thus embarked on many years slogging away at one-night performances. That he never gave less than his best is testified by Rex Graham who toured briefly with Malcolm. In a letter to him in February 2006, Rex Graham recalled one particular night.

> It must have been around the 1972 period. We had a week's tour up north working the clubs. At one, I think it was a British Legion Club, Colin Boardman who I managed was around 17 years old. He did his magic act with doves and white rabbit etc and had done his half-hour spot. I was next, comedy audience participation give-away act. After the break you took over the second half. After a couple of numbers a power cut happened. The lights went out with only the emergency ones staying on. No organ or mic, but being the showman you are, you got down off the stage and walked slowly around the club, singing without any accompaniment. You did your whole act and you brought the house down.

22

TRAVELLING MAN

Scunthorpe, Birmingham, Palmers Green, Porthcawl, Nottingham, Wolverhampton.

The summer of 1973 came as a relief from all the pounding up and down motorways. Malcolm was able to settle for twenty-one weeks in Blackpool. Peter Webster presented *Those Good Old Days* at the Central Pier in which Malcolm starred alongside Wyn Calvin. It was his first summer season as a solo artist for many years. The long English summer season show was still in full swing. Spread about the other two piers, Opera House and the Grand Theatre throughout the summer among many others were Danny La Rue, Ben Warriss and Clinton Ford.

Gaye Vaughan recalls that during the Blackpool season Malcolm suffered again the formation of kidney stones. The pain was almost unbearable but he never missed a performance and managed to keep going by drinking copious amounts of water.

Malcolm himself has recorded that with perfect timing nature took its course with one of the stones while at home just after the summer season had finished.

Dublin, Sunderland, Birkenhead, Crewe, Margate, Stoke-on-Trent, Billingham.

The occasional television appearance cropped up including a 1974 showing on a weekly favourite, *Stars on Sunday* with Jess Yates. Short tours abroad also continued as, for example, a trip to Naples under the auspices of the United Nations. The late autumn of 1974 found Malcolm in Scotland for two weeks immediately preceding pantomime in Southampton for John Farrow and Mervyn Conn.

Northampton, Workington, Bridlington, Hull, Skegness, Bristol, Rhyl.

The one-nighters kept Malcolm in the public eye throughout 1975, which was as well for nothing else did. There was no summer season that year nor a pantomime.

The summer of 1976 found Malcolm back in Jersey by courtesy of both Dick Ray and Duggie Chapman. The former was preoccupied with the Opera House that year, his first as its owner where he set up for the summer a production of *Boeing Boeing,* booking Richard O'Sullivan to star.

Duggie Chapman produced *The Good Old Days* at Swanson's Music Hall. The brothers Tommy and Harry Swanson were businessmen and life-long residents of Jersey. While Harry owned the Watersplash, one of Tommy's enterprises was a hotel named after him that stood close to the harbour and Liberation Square in St Helier. He devised and set aside a large room for entertainment and it was at such venue that Malcolm spent another eighteen weeks. Tommy Swanson was a decidedly hands-on man and Gaye recalls that whenever she saw him, he invariably carried a hammer and screwdriver with him. In fact Tommy was so often wearing overalls that he was taken for the odd-job man rather than the owner.

Jersey had become a meaningful fixture in the lives of the Vaughans, most of all because they had met on the island, and Gaye was delighted to be back. Not that it was possible to spend the entire summer there, given that she was by then a working woman and could use only her holiday entitlement to stay with her husband. Daryl and Damon were still at school or college and could therefore spend much of their long summer holiday with their father.

The Good Old Days also featured veteran comedian George Williams, famous for his mournful cry: 'I'm not well'. The music hall chairman was Alan Martin, and his wife Vivien Day also featured. Malcolm's musical director Gary Lloyd was there along with Mike Jamieson, billed as The Music Men. Female impersonator Bobbie Kent and 'the Gorgeous Gaiety Girls' with Mary Carrell completed the cast.

Daryl Vaughan was by then nineteen years old and showing signs of interest in the technical side of theatre. Dick Ray allowed him his head and Daryl set about the lighting design of *The Good Old Days.* He received further work from Dick Ray who enlisted him as a driver for Sunday evenings when he transported dancers from the weekday show to various venues around Jersey for special concerts.

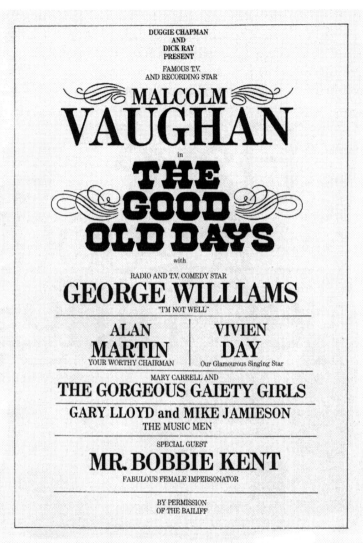

Summer 1976

The Vaughans were aware that work in the business was becoming increasingly erratic. There was still a family and a mortgage to maintain. 1977 was a year of considerable change in both their working lives. Following his journey to Workington and appearance in the town on 31 January, Malcolm decided to try his luck on his doorstep.

A front-of-house job became available at the Streatham Hill Theatre. It was but a short distance from his West Norwood home and he would be back with his family. It did not prove to be the answer. The job was designed as part of a management training course with Mecca and the intention was that Malcolm would be given charge of the company's bingo hall at Camberwell. It was a different clientele yet one that sometimes persuaded him to give them a song.

Within a short time Malcolm sank into depression and lasted no more than a few months in his new work. At the same time Gaye embarked on a part-time career for herself. With Malcolm no longer self-employed, she ceased to be his secretary when taken on by the Department of Employment at the Holborn Job Centre. As the year progressed and Malcolm's foray into theatre management turned to dust, Gaye saw the need to go full-time, which she did for the following seventeen years. It was a case of grinning and bearing it for by her own admission she did not enjoy the work. All her previous employment from an early age had been in the private sector, whose conditions applied also to Malcolm's career. Now she was able to see daily, as she concluded, the waste in government service and the propensity of its workers to 'throw sickies'. The lackadaisical attitude to work in general was entirely alien to her ethos.

Meanwhile they both suggested that Malcolm try to stick to what he knew best. On 15 October he made a return to the clubs with a date organised by Reg Summerfield, an agent based in the Midlands. He obtained for Malcolm an engagement at a club at Drumchapel near Glasgow for £250. Because it was another first and a potentially uncertain time, Gaye travelled with Malcolm to Scotland to see him through it. Malcolm had a good reception and they came home on the Sunday so that Gaye could return to her uninspiring job on the Monday morning. Malcolm got back into the swing of his trade and soldiered on in the business. At the end of the same year he performed in pantomime for two weeks at Barrow-in-Furness.

So it was on the road again. Glasgow, Leominster, Purley, Batley, Norwich, Plymouth.

The summer of 1978 provided another respite from the travelling with a return to summer season at Clacton's West Cliff Theatre for

Francis Golightly. Malcolm completed fourteen weeks at the end of September.

While at Clacton Malcolm signed a contract with the Theatre Royal, Newcastle to appear in *Aladdin* the following Christmas. Rehearsals would begin on 4 December and the pantomime would open on 16 December. He would be paid at the rate of £50 per week for the rehearsal period and then at £325 per week for the duration of the show. The contract stipulated: 'To perform the part of The Vizier and understudy Dickie Henderson.' The pantomime ran until 1 February 1979.

Midlands, Surrey, Isle of Man, Scotland, Oxford, six concerts for Butlins.

The one-nighters provided the mainstay for 1979 and it was during a visit to the Villa Marina that Malcolm gave an interview to Radio Isle of Man. He provided an insight into how he felt about his craft despite the travelling. It came in an answer when he was asked if he enjoyed television.

'Not really. I prefer live work. On television you do things over and over again before recording. It gets boring, repetitive and it's tiring on the throat. On the other hand it's essential for exposure. But in live work it's people, it's seeing people in front of you. It's the atmosphere of flesh and blood there.'

The family decided they were in need of a substantial break. Malcolm's work was fairly regular and Gaye was established in the Civil Service. Despite interest in stage lighting, a field to which he would return in later years, Daryl had decided to join British Airways. He was able to arrange concessionary flights for the whole family's first visit to the United States.

They flew to Los Angeles. The first thing that happened to them was to find David Frost waiting among the crowd at the arrival hall. Even the usually unruffled television host was startled when Malcolm marched up to him, said hello and announced himself. For a moment Mr Frost clearly wondered if this was the man he was there to meet. In their two-week trip they established themselves in the New Century Inn. Malcolm met up unexpectedly with two old friends, one in L.A. and the other in Las Vegas.

In a small theatre in Santa Monica they found, of all things, a season of 'Old Tyme Music Hall' in progress. Starring in it was British comedian Joe Baker who had been one half of a successful comedy act for twelve years alongside Jack Douglas. He had branched out solo and 'The Joe Baker Show' had featured on Lew Grade's ATV in the Sixties. Joe had decided to try his luck in America. Whether it was because the Vaughan family were in that night or because it was his usual style, he geared the comedy to the small contingent of British audience. In the end, Gaye recalls, it was embarrassing because they were the only four who understood Joe Baker's humour and were therefore the only ones laughing.

Even more incongruous was the family's discovery in Las Vegas. Appearing in support at The Dunes was a comedian from the Forties and Fifties, still working his act as a baby in a playpen. It was Freddie Sales. Perhaps because his comedy was so visual, he appeared to be popular with the audience. The family crowded into his dressing room afterwards in time to see a snippet of the Oscars when someone from Malcolm's early working days received a lifetime achievement award. Malcolm's thoughts went swiftly back thirty-five years to being directed in London in *The Skin of Our Teeth* as he watched Laurence Olivier receiving the statuette from Cary Grant, and managing to mangle his emotional acceptance speech with phrases such as 'the top of this moment'. Jon Voigt in the theatre audience had been primed by the producers to provide the cameras with a meaningful reaction shot.

During their stay Malcolm continued to let others do the entertaining, especially when they went to the Desert Inn and the glory of Juliet Prowse teamed with Anthony Newley.

Back at home Malcolm's batteries were recharged to get on the road again. So it was Weymouth, Lincoln, Bournemouth, Weston-Super-Mare, Manchester, Yarmouth. And so forth.

By 1980 Malcolm was beginning to make comments against his itinerary. His records therefore show examples such as: Lewisham – good; South Acton Working Men's Club – tickets too high at £2; Birmingham – great; Richmond Place Club, Hereford – so so; Stechford Social Club – v v good; Rushall Labour Club – can't remember; Slough Town Football Club – v v v good, packed, standing ovation; Southampton – (car accident), throat very bad; Neath – never ever again.'

Between 1 April and 24 April 1982 Malcolm appeared somewhere different every night and always drove back to Cheviot Road, Streatham, often not arriving until four o'clock in the morning. The process was starting to take its toll.

Pantomime was drying up fast, his last taking place at Bexhill-on-Sea for no more than two weeks at Christmas 1980.

Coventry, Burton-on-Trent, Walsall, Gloucester, Southsea.

The signs were in place. Malcolm was getting to the end of the road. There was one summer season to go, and one replete with irony. On 3 July 1982 he starred in a four-week season for Bernard Parr. It was to be his last and it took place at Morecambe, the scene of his first summer season nearly forty years earlier when as the boy Malcolm Thomas he had appeared with Michael Austin, Tommy Reilly and Hal Monty.

At the end of the run, Malcolm Vaughan never worked in show business again. And yet in the ensuing years show business had a knack of not leaving him alone.

*Dave Allen helps Malcolm celebrate his 40th wedding anniversary,
June, 1996.*

*Producer Johnny Mans encourages Malcolm to pick a raffle ticket
at the 'Encore' Theatre Awards Lunch, May 2006.*

Malcolm is reunited with Rosemary Squires following her show with Jeff Hooper, Winter Garden, Eastbourne, 2006.

Malcolm at his Golden Wedding celebration with lifelong friend Peter Killick and the author, Grand Hotel, Eastbourne, Saturday 17 June 2006.

Malcolm and Gaye celebrate their Golden Wedding, June, 2006.
(photo: Eastbourne Herald)

Malcolm outside the Watersplash, Jersey, now a surfing centre, April, 2007.

Gaye and Malcolm return to Plemont Bay, Jersey, where they had met 52 years earlier, April 2007.

Judy, Daryl and Zachary Vaughan

Malcolm's grandchildren – l to r: Emma, Alice and Zachary

l to r: Zachary, Gaye, Alice, Emma and Malcolm – 2004

Damon, Lynda, Emma, Alice, Gaye and Malcolm at Dizzy's Jazz Club, Manhattan, 2005

23

A BUSY AUTUMN

Enough was enough. The constant traipsing up and down the country came to a stop when Malcolm Vaughan left show business after the end of the summer season at Morecambe in 1982. But where to now? The disastrous experience of five years earlier had shown him he could not face trying front-of-house work again. That autumn provided a series of trials in several senses of the word. He looked at the possibility of becoming a representative for a book-buying company in Croydon. There was the store in Charing Cross Road that needed someone to create computer pictures from original photographs, which Malcolm tried for a while.

The Brixton Employment Office put him in touch with a careers advisor at the City branch who suggested that he try insurance sales. After all, he had been selling his own talent for years. An element of straw-clutching seems to have been the motive of the advisor. 1982 was a time when a cycle of unemployment was beginning to take hold. A considerable pruning was taking place in the public sector and would eventually spread to the private. It was not the best of times for someone of fifty-three with only a talent for singing to be unemployed. The future looked bleak. Yet rescue came through persistence and a spotted advertisement that would take Malcolm in an entirely different direction.

There was in the 1980s a body called the Central Medical Establishment. Based in Cleveland Street, London, it dealt with the medical problems of members of all armed services. Because of the continuing terrorist threat from the Irish Republican Army at the time, the building was *incognito*. The front entrance was nondescript and there was no suggestion as to the building's use. A receptionist was needed. Malcolm applied for the job and was successful. He started working there on 10 January 1983 and stayed for eleven years until his official retirement age in 1994.

Malcolm claims that it proved to be one of the happiest periods of his life. He met a succession of service personnel and always enjoyed dealing with them. Some recognised him and much conversation was struck up.

Gaye reflects that his salary of £11,000 per year probably did not represent a quarter of his potential earnings in show business. In her own words: 'Mal could earn in one night what he was paid in a month at the CME. But that one night could be the only one in three weeks.' Her relief, therefore, lay in the recognition that it was regular and could be relied upon. Financially she felt far more secure than she had been through all the years of never knowing whether there would be a pay cheque beyond the end of the current job. The advantages to the new situation were thus apparent to both of them, but there was a downside. Malcolm Vaughan never sang in public again.

'It was upsetting,' says Gaye. 'I had known nights when people had stood and cheered his performances. I suppose it was a touch of reflected glory but I missed all that so much. And apart from my feelings it seemed such a waste for him not to be using that beautiful voice any more.'

Malcolm himself took a different, even complacent, view. He did not in the least miss getting up on a stage with a microphone. His older son, Daryl Vaughan, believes that his father never really had any ambition while in the business. If a job came his way it was gravy and there was money to put down on the family kitchen table.

There is some evidence to back up Daryl's view. Going back fifty years to *The British Record Star Show* at the London Palladium, critic Robert Wraight can be found noting in his review a contrast in attitude between Malcolm and a fellow performer.

For me (one of) the evening's highlights came from Malcolm Vaughan, a young man with a pleasant voice that he refuses to take seriously. In this he is very different from David Whitfield who shares with his fans so much respect for his own voice that he has his own musical director to take over the orchestra while he sings.

In an article in the monthly magazine *Hit Parade* in January 1957 the unnamed writer observed the strongly realistic approach in the singer. With all the success surrounding 'St Therese of the Roses',

Malcolm looked on elated, but he is too hardened to the see-saw of show business to allow it to make him float on air too much. Having seen every angle of it, he has no starry-eyed illusions about it all.

No example of his philosophy could have been bettered than with his own words in an interview for *TV Mirror and Disc News* in June 1957.

You know what this music business is. You're as good as your last hit record. I'll tell you something. A few months back we did the tour with Bill Haley and his Comets. We did fantastic business all over the place. But even now Haley isn't so big as he was then. And if a million-dollar concern can slip like that, how much easier could it happen to me?

Gaye Vaughan has a theory about Malcolm's priority that his family would always come first. She feels that the loss of his mother at such a young and vulnerable age made him determined to have as many of the best years of his life as possible built around his own marriage and the precious issue arising from it.

It follows that there was never a burning passion to take Carnegie Hall by storm. Which helped considerably in his adjustment to work outside the business when the time came, and which entrenched him in his determination not to return to it.

Only one incident had him faltering: the offer of a pantomime during the six months of his probationary period at the Central Medical Establishment. He consulted his commandant about the likelihood of being kept on in the job. Although unable to commit himself the officer said there was indeed a strong likelihood. On the strength of that, Malcolm Vaughan made the decision to turn down the offer of the pantomime, and the seal was set on his parting with show business for good.

Yet show business seemed determined not to part with Malcolm Vaughan. For example, in December 1983 a long-playing record of his hits was released. Together with his salary at the Central Medical Establishment some useful royalties continued to come his way.

The following year saw a further house removal. The Vaughans decided to move to Sanderstead and it was between there and London that they commuted every day to their respective Civil Service jobs, from which in 1994 they both retired.

In 1997 EMI released the CD 'The Magic of Malcolm Vaughan'. On the compilation are all the hits together with a moving rendition of Rodgers and Hammerstein's 'Hello Young Lovers', a song not often associated with a male singer but here executed to perfection. The one song accompanied by piano only is 'If You Were the Only Girl in The World', giving especial emphasis to the unique Vaughan sound. All other tracks receive the treatment of the full orchestra and stirring arrangements of its conductor, Frank Cordell, who had gone on to a separate career in composing movie scores. One of these was the blended complexity of the work for the 1970 film, *Cromwell,* with Richard Harris in the title role. Several years earlier Cordell had been in the strong running to be the composer for David Lean's *Lawrence of Arabia.* He was pipped at the post by Maurice Jarre. Also included among the twenty-five tracks of the CD are the subtle standard 'My Foolish Heart' and Malcolm's inspiring 1961 version of 'The Wedding'.

At the turn of the Millennium news arrived out of the blue that Malcolm was being featured on the soundtrack of a new movie. He and Gaye were made aware of it at the New Year while taking a holiday in Cape Town with long-standing friends Pam and Peter Killick and their son Paul. They received a telephone call from Damon Vaughan who tipped them off that a film had been made in which Malcolm's singing voice was being used. There had been no prior notice given to Malcolm.

It was William Trevor's novel, *Felicia's Journey,* which had been filmed by Icon Productions starring Bob Hoskins. The story goes that producer Bruce Davey was on his way to the studios one day and was talking about his project to his taxi driver. He said he was thinking of using the voice of Peggy Lee for the purpose intended. They chatted at some length and then the driver apparently asked: 'Have you thought about using the voice of Malcolm Vaughan?' Bruce Davey had not heard the name before. On looking further into the matter he was persuaded.

In *Felicia's Journey* – possibly one of the bleakest films ever made – Bob Hoskins' character is seen to have a pre-occupation with the records of Malcolm Vaughan, though Malcolm's name is never mentioned. On the screen, however, is a shot of Hoskins taking a long-playing record from a sleeve that clearly sports a large photograph of Malcolm in his heyday. As the credits begin to roll at the opening the voice of Malcolm singing 'The Heart of a Child' is heard. At various times through the film the audience also hears Malcolm's renditions of 'My Special Angel' and 'More Than Ever'.

In 2001 Malcolm and Gaye Vaughan moved once more, from Sanderstead to their present home in Eastbourne. One Sunday afternoon, following a drive to Brighton, they were on their way home as Ed Stewart was broadcasting his programme on BBC Radio 2. A record was being played featuring Joan Regan. When it finished, Ed Stewart asked listeners if they knew who the accompanying pianist was. In unison Gaye and Malcolm observed that it was Russ Conway, which was confirmed by Stewart. Immediately Gaye thought up the idea that it would be interesting to discover what had happened to various artists who had largely disappeared from the radar. She suggested to Malcolm that he contact Ed Stewart to introduce himself and suggest a phone-in with the programme's host. Stewart took it up and Malcolm was the first artist to be so interviewed.

The tram was set in motion and for some time thereafter Ed Stewart reserved a spot on the show in which he made contact with performers, who included Russ Conway and Freddie Garrity, interviewing each and playing their chosen music.

The Vaughans have taken to life in Eastbourne where they enjoy an active retirement. Both attend gym classes and they launch into lengthy walks along the seafront in spite of Malcolm's progressive health problems, casting him ever further into the darkness of Alzheimer's disease. They have joined the many folk from show business who have traditionally settled in the south coast town, thereby enabling them to renew acquaintance with some of Malcolm's erstwhile colleagues. Apart from choreographer Jan Lynton they include the Plummers, once known as Tommy Wallis and Beryl (the latter a recent Queen Ratling), producer Robert Marlowe, singer/actress Jacquie Toye and her musical director husband, Paul Davis.

All of these and more, including Mr and Mrs Kenneth Earle, came together at the Grand Hotel, Eastbourne on Saturday 17 June 2006 to help celebrate the Golden Wedding anniversary of Gaye and Malcolm Vaughan.

Kenneth and Carol Earle were accompanied by the man who had given a boost to the Earle & Vaughan act and then gone on to succeed in the provision of alternative comedy in London. Don Ward first met Earle & Vaughan at the Watersplash, Jersey in the 1960s. He was working as a comic at Pontins Holiday Camp, the same where Gaye and Malcolm had met when it was still Parkins Camp. Ward would frequently call in at the Watersplash to watch the act. In 1968 he saw the pair work at the Playboy Club in London and the following winter, when Earle & Vaughan were in pantomime at the Golders

Green Hippodrome, he booked them to appear late-night at the Gargoyle Club. Don Ward was introducing comedy to the Club, taking something of a risk with what was a striptease venue. He included many young comedians who were being given the opportunity to air their talents, including Alexei Sayle and French & Saunders. Because of the venture's success, Ward went on to set up the Comedy Store, opposite the Prince of Wales Theatre, Oxendon Street.

Also present at the Golden Wedding celebration was a direct link with the Vaughans' first date: singer and actress Olivia Breeze. Malcolm had made the first telephone call to invite Gaye out from backstage at the Granada, Tooting in the autumn of 1955. It was during the week he was appearing in *The Billy Cotton Band Show,* whose lead vocalist was Olivia's father, Alan Breeze.

It was possible for only one of the Vaughan sons, Damon, to attend the Golden Wedding. Both he and brother Daryl now live in different parts of the United States and are established with their own families. When the celebration was over, Gaye and Malcolm made one of their occasional visits to first Texas and then New Jersey to see their grandchildren.

Anyone who comes into long-standing contact with Gaye and Malcolm Vaughan recognises that their partnership, which first saw the light of day in the summer of 1955, has been an enduring example of devotion.

In the last analysis it is probably the essence of family life, consistently uppermost in his priorities, which always rendered Malcolm Vaughan a reluctant star.

MALCOLM VAUGHAN
DISCOGRAPHY

Malcolm Vaughan's recording career spanned some nine years, from 1955 to 1963. During this period he was signed exclusively to the HMV music label and he recorded over fifty songs. The early recordings were released on 78rpm 'shellac' discs before giving way to the newer 45rpm vinyl singles in the mid-fifties. A total of six 45rpm 'EPs' were added to the roster, along with one 33rpm 'LP'. All the recordings took place at EMI's famed Abbey Road studios. Although never reaching the coveted No.1 slot, Malcolm enjoyed a total of 106 weeks in the UK charts, eclipsing many of his contemporaries. It remains an enviable achievement in the fickle world of popular music, even to this day. In the years since 1963, as a testament to his enduring popularity with the record buying public, a considerable number of compilation albums have been released by HMV, and their parent company EMI. These have appeared on a range of formats, from vinyl albums and compact cassettes to audio CDs. It is believed that the following discography is a complete and accurate listing of his entire recording repertoire.

45rpm SINGLES

Date	Title A/B	Catalogue No.	Chart Position
1955	Ev'ry Day Of My Life / Mama	HMV B10874	No.5
1955	More Than A Millionaire / Take Me Back Again	HMV B10923 / HMV 7M317	
1955	With Your Love / Small Talk	HMV POP130 / HMV 7M338	No.18
1956	Only You And You Alone / I'll Be Near To You	HMV POP186 / HMV 7M389	
1956	St. Theresa Of The Roses / Love Me As Though There Were No Tomorrow	HMV POP250	
1957	The World Is Mine / Now	HMV POP303	No.3
1957	Chapel Of The Roses / Guardian Angel	HMV POP325	No.26
1957	Oh! My Papa / What Is My Destiny	HMV POP381	No.13
1958	My Special Angel / The Heart Of A Child	HMV POP419	No.3
1958	To Be Loved / My Loving Arms	HMV POP459	No.14
1958	Ev'ry Hour Ev'ry Day Of My Life / Miss You	HMV POP502	
1958	More Than Ever (Comé Prima) / A Night To Remember	HMV POP538	
1959	Wait For Me / Willingly	HMV POP590	No.5
1959	You'll Never Walk Alone / The Holy City	HMV POP687	No.13
1960	Oh So Wunderbar / For Everyone In Love	HMV POP700	
1960	My Love For You / Lady Of Spain	HMV POP739	
1961	There's No Other Love / Dolce Vita	HMV POP846	
1961	The Wedding / Guardian Angel	HMV POP923	
1963	This Side Of Heaven / The Love Of A Lifetime	HMV POP1120	

EXTENDED PLAY COMPILATIONS

Date	Title AA/BB	Catalogue No.
1957	"Sincerity In Song – Volume 1" St. Theresa Of The Roses / What Is My Destiny / Chapel Of The Roses / Ev'ry Day Of My Life	HMV 7EG8272
1958	"Sincerity In Song – Volume 2" To Be Loved / Miss You / Ev'ry Hour Ev'ry Day Of My Life / My Special Angel	HMV 7EG8377
1959	"Sincerity In Song – Volume 3" More Than Ever / Willingly / Wait For Me (Ti Diro) / The Heart Of A Child	HMV 7EG8453
1960	"Hello Malcolm Vaughan No.1" We Kiss In A Shadow / Make Believe / Hello Young Lovers / If You Were The Only Girl In The World	HMV 7EG8542 (GES5785)
1960	"Hello Malcolm Vaughan No.2" And This Is My Beloved / Look For The Silver Lining / If I Loved You / Where Or When	HMV 7EG8560 (GES5793)
1960	"Request For Malcolm Vaughan" Lady Of Spain / My Foolish Heart / The Night Is Young / South of the Border	HMV 7EG8579 (GES5799)

ALBUMS

Date	*Title / Track Listing*	*Catalogue No.*

1959 'Hello, Malcolm Vaughan'   LP: HMV – CLP1284

1   We Kiss in A Shadow
2   Make Believe
3   Hello Young Lovers
4   Vilia
5   April Showers
6   You'll Never Walk Alone
7   Where or When
8   Look For The Silver Lining
9   One Alone
10   If You Were The Only Girl In The World
11   And This Is My Beloved
12   If I Loved You

1977 'The Best Of Malcolm Vaughan'

LP: EMI One Up – OU2043

1   More Than Ever
2   St. Theresa Of The Roses
3   The Wedding
4   Oh My Papa (O Mein Papa)
5   Ev'ry Day Of My Life
6   Wait For Me (Ti Diro)
7   To Be Loved
8   What Is My Destiny
9   Chapel Of The Roses
10   My Special Angel
11   Miss You
12   La Dolce Vita
13   My Foolish Heart
14   Mama
15   Guardian Angel
16   If You Were The Only Girl In The World

1984 'The Very Best Of Malcolm Vaughan'

LP: EMI *Music For Pleasure*
EMI MFP 4156471

1   My Special Angel
2   Wait For Me (Ti Diro)
3   Only You (And You Alone)
4   With Your Love (Mes Mains)
5   Oh My Papa (O Mein Papa)
6   The World Is Mine
7   If You Were The Only Girl In The World
8   More Than Ever
9   St. Theresa Of The Roses
10 Ev'ry Day Of My Life
11 Miss You
12 Willingly (Melodie Perdue)
13 Chapel Of The Roses
14 Hello Young Lovers
15 To Be Loved
16 You'll Never Walk Alone

1990 'The Best Of Malcolm Vaughan – The EMI Years'

LP: EMS 1358
Cassette: TC – EMI 1358
CD: CDP 7941432

1   My Special Angel
2   Mama
3   With Your Love (Mes Mains)
4   Love Me As Though There Were No Tomorrow
5   Lady Of Spain
6   More Than Ever
7   Wait For Me (Ti Diro)
8   You'll Never Walk Alone
9   St. Theresa Of The Roses
10 To Be Loved
11 The Heart Of A Child

12	Chapel Of The Roses
13	The Wedding
14	Ev'ry Day Of My Life
15	The World Is Mine
16	The Holy City

1997   'EMI Presents The Magic Of Malcolm Vaughan'

Cassette: TC – MFP 6289

CD: CD – MFP 6289

1	Chapel Of The Roses
2	Ev'ry Day Of My Life
3	More Than Ever
4	My Special Angel
5	St. Theresa Of The Roses
6	To Be Loved
7	Wait For Me (Ti Diro)
8	With Your Love (Mes Mains)
9	The World Is Mine
10	Hello Young Lovers
11	The Heart Of A Child
12	The Holy City
13	Lady Of Spain
14	Love Me As Though There Were No Other
15	The Wedding
16	You'll Never Walk Alone
17	Only You (And You Alone)
18	Oh My Papa (O Mein Papa)
19	If You Were The Only Girl In The World
20	Miss You
21	Willingly (Melodie Perdue)
22	A Bell Is Ringing
23	My Foolish Heart
24	Guardian Angel
25	When The Last Rose Has Faded

2008   **'The Very Best Of Malcolm Vaughan'**
EMI Gold Double CD: 226 7602

Disc One

1   St. Theresa Of The Roses
2   Ev'ry Day Of My Life
3   And This Is My Beloved
4   Make Believe
5   Chapel Of The Roses
6   The Love Of A Lifetime
7   I'll Be Near You
8   Mama
9   Hello Young Lovers
10 La Dolce Vita
11 My Foolish Heart
12 Now
13 Lady Of Spain
14 Guardian Angel
15 My Love For You
16 There's No Other Love
17 To Be Loved
18 Only You (And You Alone)
19 South Of The Border
20 Vilia
21 When The Last Rose Has Faded
22 This Side Of Heaven
23 The Heart Of A Child
24 Wait For Me (Ti Diro)
25 I'd Never Forgive Myself

Disc Two

1   Look For The Silver Lining
2   Miss You
3   My Special Angel
4   More Than Ever
5   Oh My Papa (O Mein Papa)

6   If I Loved You
7   Love Me As Though There Were No Tomorrow
8   Oh So Wunderbar
9   The Night Is Young And You're So Beautiful
10   One Alone
11   If You Were The Only Girl In The World
12   The Wedding
13   We Kiss in A Shadow
14   What Is My Destiny
15   A Night To Remember
16   Willingly (Melodie Perdue)
17   More Than A Millionaire
18   Where Or When
19   The World Is Mine
20   You'll Never Walk Alone
21   Take Me Back Again
22   With Your Love (Mes Mains)
23   Small Talk
24   Ev'ry Hour Ev'ry Day Of My Life
25   My Loving Arms

Songs recorded but never released:

Any Time
For Everyone in Love
I'd Never Forgive Myself
The Last Mile Home
No Other Love
A Silhouette In Lovers Lane
The World Outside
Until Now

INDEX

Jacobs, David, 108
James, Jimmy, 8
Jamieson, Mike, 140
Jenny Jones, 7-9, 13, 15-17, 19, 74, 75
Jimmy Wheeler Show, The, 67
Johns, Bambi, 47
Johns, Barry, 46, 47
Johns, Bernard, 46, 47
Johns, Maggie, 47
Johnson, Bryan, 67, 108
Johnson, Cecil, 45
Johnson, Teddy, 1, 66
Junk Junction, 15, 16
Junkin, John, 137

K

Kaye Sisters, The, 73
Keene, Marion, 67
Kent, Bobbie, 140
Killick, Pamela, 156
Killick, Paul, 156
Killick, Peter, 156
King, Dave, 74, 75
King, Evan, 44
Kitt, Eartha, 85
Konyot, Marion, 118
Konyots, The, 118

L

'La Dolce Vita', 119
'Lady of Spain', 109
Lancaster, Pat, 8
Lane, Arthur, 25
Lane, Desmond, 87, 124
Lane, Marian, 53
Lang, Don, 95
Lanza, Mario, 1, 54, 99
'Last Rose Has Faded, The', 56
Laugh Town Laugh, 19, 20, 22, 41
Lawrence, Douglas, 73

Lee, Max, 46
Leigh, Vivien, 27
Leslie, Cynthia, 52
Lewis, Kevin, 120, 122, 123, 135
Lewis, J, 44
Lewis, Vic, 87, 88
Lloyd, Gary, 138, 140
Lockwood, Margaret, 26
Long, William, 3
Lord, Walter, 106
Lotis, Denis, 1
Lotis, Denis, Mrs, 98
Lotus and Josie, 53
'Love Me As Though There Were No Tomorrow', 72
'Love of a Lifetime, The', 120
Lovell, Raymond, 30
Lucan, Arthur, 49, 51
Lunch Box, 102
Lune, Ted, 120
Lynne, Carole (Lady Delfont), 8
Lynton, Jan (Janice Peeling), 134-136, 158

M

MacQuitty, William, 105
'Magic of Malcolm Vaughan, The', 156
'Mama', 55
Man's Affair, A, 40
Marlowe, Robert, 158
Marsden, Betty, 25
Martin, Alan, 140
Martin-Davies, Edith, 13, 15
Mason, Don, 73
Mason, Glen, 67, 95
Mayne, Bill, 49, 51, 52
McCormack, John, 100, 106
McCormick, John, 30, 31
McCrindle, Alex, 32